THE BATTLE IS GOD'S

The Battle is God's

REFLECTING ON SPIRITUAL
WARFARE FOR AFRICAN BELIEVERS

Keith Ferdinando

AFRICA CHRISTIAN TEXTBOOKS

2012

The Battle is God's
© 2012 by Keith Ferdinando

Africa Christian Textbooks (ACTS)

ACTS Bookshop, International HQ, TCNN,
PMB 2020, Bukuru, Plateau State, 930008, Nigeria
GSM: +234 (0) 803-589-5328; E-mail: acts.jos@gmail.com
Website: http://www.acts-ng.com

ISBN: 978-978-905-143-4 Print
ISBN: 978-978-905-228-8 ePub
ISBN: 978-978-905-229-5 Mobi

ACTS has 11 branches:

Abuja (Garki, International Market)	0703 771 2858
Ilorin (UMCA)	0803 208 4031
Jos (JETS)	0803 923 4762
Jos (TCNN)	0803 946 8691
Kagoro (ETS)	0802 798 4408
Lagos (Ikeja, Underbridge Bus Stop)	0803 218 0523
Lagos (WATS)	0802 367 0628
Ogbomoso (NBTS)	0803 536 8021
Saminaka (TSNN)	0813 125 1284
Uyo (Obio Imo St)	0802 784 3266
Kenya (NEGST)	acts.kenya@gmail.com

To my wife Margaret,
a woman who fears the Lord

'This is what the LORD says to you: "Do not be afraid or discouraged because of this vast army. For the battle is not yours, but God's".'

—2 Chronicles 20:15

CONTENTS

PREFACE

The reality of Christian living is always one of spiritual conflict: believers are members of the church militant, and they are in serious danger if they forget it. The purpose of the present study is to reflect on the nature of spiritual combat in the African context. Of course, because humanity is essentially the same in every age and place – created in God's image, fallen, in need of redemption – as are sin, Satan, the world and the gospel of grace, much that is said here should be always and everywhere true. However, there are also distinct issues that emerge from the particularity of the cultural context, and to these special attention must be given. It is the purpose of this study to reflect on issues of spiritual warfare which African culture raises, while setting them in the context of the overriding themes of such warfare that characterise every time and place.

Some of the content presented here is drawn from my thesis, which was published in 1999,[1] but it has been very substantially reshaped and broadened, and most of the apparatus of footnotes and bibliography has been removed. A major goal has been to make the main argument of the earlier work accessible to many more people, and consequently more widely useful. As I have tried to draw the threads together, I have greatly benefited from numerous opportunities of discussing the subject with students and colleagues in varying

---

[1] K. Ferdinando, *The Triumph of Christ in African Perspective: a Study of Demonology and Redemption in the African Context* (Carlisle: Paternoster, 1999).

African contexts – especially in Chad, DR Congo and Angola – and I am greatly indebted to them all.

I wish to thank my niece, Miss Rachel Hull, for her excellent work on the cover design, and also Dr Paul Todd of Africa Christian Textbooks for overseeing the publication of the book. I am also most grateful to Miss Ailish Eves and Dr Richard Gehman, highly esteemed friends and colleagues, for reading an early draft of the work and making many useful suggestions for its improvement. The resulting book is better for their contribution, while all remaining faults are my own alone.

FOREWORD

Oftentimes, discussions on spiritual warfare either focus exclusively on providing biblical proof texts without serious reflection on the cultural context, or simply overemphasise the cultural realities of demonic attacks with little or no biblical interaction. Dr. Keith Ferdinando avoids both extremes. The author's purpose is to "reflect on the nature of spiritual combat in the African context" (preface, ix). He does this in following a carefully argued presentation, looking at the role of culture and human reality, the African worldview, the Bible and the unseen world, the victory of Christ, salvation and struggle, and the weapons of Christian warfare.

Dr. Ferdinando argues correctly that every human society has a culture, and all human beings grow up within the context of their culture and are significantly shaped by it. There is no such thing as a culture-free person. Culture fashions the way in which people think and determines what is normal and proper for them (2). Within the traditional African worldview, beliefs in spirits and sorcerers have been used to explain the presence and causes of misfortune, and how to respond appropriately.

The Bible affirms the existence of an invisible spiritual realm, populated by an immense variety of divinely created spirit beings who influence what happens on earth. Satan is the supreme enemy of God and all his works. This invisible cosmos and its relationship with human beings is ruled by a sovereign, loving and good God. The apparent fixation of the traditional African worldview with spirits, witchcraft and sorcery, is in sharp contrast to this biblical reticence (51)

In all of these realities, no truth is more important than the victory that Christ accomplishes over all the powers of evil. The most decisive combat took place at the cross where Jesus broke the power of the evil one over lost human beings, and did so by bearing their sins in his sacrificial death. As a result, believers participate already in the triumph that Christ has won for them: they have even now overcome the dragon "by the blood of the lamb" (Rev. 12:11). The conflict is real but victory is assured (76).

Believers face a struggle with the world, the flesh and the devil. However, it is not a struggle that determines whether or not they will finally be saved. Rather, it is a struggle that takes place because they have already been saved through the death and resurrection of Jesus Christ. Moreover, it is one in which they have the assurance of his constant presence and of the indwelling power of the Holy Spirit in their lives to guide and sustain them.

Spiritual warfare is the conflict Christians and churches must wage with sin, the world and the devil. They would not know this conflict if God himself had not redeemed them. In that sense, it is an evidence of their salvation so that they may actually take heart from it.

The church must use spiritual weapons in its collective life and ministry, shaped by the Scriptures and not by the surrounding culture of the world. Ultimately, the battle is always God's. Evil never ever wins. Christians must take heart, for Christ has overcome the world (John 16:33) (135).

The author has scratched where the African believer is itching. Dr. Ferdinando provides deep insights into the African worldview. He delves into the theological and philosophical issues of the problem of pain and suffering and how to overcome spiritual battles by presenting solutions that are anchored in Scripture and sound evangelical theology. This is a must read for all African Bible teachers, students, pastors and believers who need to grasp the serious and complex nature of spiritual struggles and how to be victorious.

Rev Professor Samuel Waje Kunhiyop, PhD
General Secretary, Evangelical Church Winning All (ECWA).

And when I think of how,
at Calvary,
he bore sin's penalty
instead of me,
amazed, I wonder why
he, the sinless One, should die
for one so vile as I:
my Saviour He!

Now all my heart's desire
is to abide
in him, my Saviour dear,
in Him to hide.
My shield and buckler He,
covering and protecting me:
from Satan's darts I'll be
safe at His side.

Lord Jesus, hear my prayer,
your grace impart;
when evil thoughts arise
through Satan's art,
O, drive them all away
and my God, from day to day,
keep me beneath your sway,
King of my heart. [1]

---

[1] E. T. Sibomana, 'O how the grace of God amazes me', translated by R. Guillebaud, in Brian Edwards et al (eds.), *Praise! Psalms, Hymns and Songs for Christian Worship* (Darlington: Praise Trust, 2000), 749.

CHAPTER 1

CULTURE AND TRANSFORMATION

"Now was the opportunity," I thought, as I sat in the school classroom. The teacher had finally opened up a general discussion time with the class to discuss various philosophical issues. I lifted my hand to raise the question which had puzzled me for some time. Taking a deep breath, I asked, "How do I know that the world around me is actually real?" The look on the teacher's face and the tittering of the other students showed me that I had not been understood, so I repeated my question. "How do I know that the world is really there and is not merely a projection in my own mind, like some film, which will one day come to an end?" The class erupted into laughter. The teacher politely said that the world is there because all our senses confirm the fact, and then moved onto another topic. ...

Years later, I journeyed to the great land of India and there met with a Hindu guru sitting lotus-style dressed in a simple cloth. When I asked him my question he smiled knowingly, and acknowledged the insight behind my words. Why did the guru have such a different response to my question? As I began to understand the complexities of Indian culture, I began to understand the major differences in the assumptions which exist between the West and the East. These differences have in recent years been called 'worldview', by behavioural scientists. I began to comprehend how important this concept was not just for understanding the thinking of another people, but in grasping the assumptions of my own culture and my own Christian beliefs.[1]

Every human society has a culture, and all human beings grow up within the context of their culture and are significantly shaped by it. There is no such thing as a culture-free person. At the same time, cultures are human creations. Men and women collectively – and largely unconsciously – shape and modify the culture of their society, and in numerous ways pass on its beliefs and practices to their children. There is thus a reciprocal relationship between culture and human beings: culture moulds people, but is itself a product of human ingenuity and creativity.

Culture fashions the way in which all those who share it live and think. It determines what they regard as normal and proper, and it influences almost every aspect of their lives. For example, culture tells people how they should relate to one another, whether in the marriage relationship, child-rearing practices, or attitudes towards those of other societies and cultures. Culture defines the types of work people do, as well as the status and rewards associated with each job. Culture determines the types of building people live in, as well as their construction and meaning. It prescribes the clothes people wear, the materials used to make them, and – once again – the meanings attached to different types of clothing. Culture

---

[1] D. Burnett, *Clash of Worlds* (Crowborough: Marc, 1990), 11-12. Reproduced by permission of Lion Hudson plc., Oxford, U.K.

specifies the food people eat, how they find and prepare it, and what foods are appropriate to particular groups within the society or for particular occasions. In short, the total culture of any society can be defined quite simply as their "design for living."[2]

Many factors combine to give each culture its own unique shape. Among these are the local climate and ecology, the level of technological sophistication reached by the society, the degree of interaction with other peoples, the religious beliefs held by the people, and human creativity itself. Moreover, cultures are always in a state of change, which can sometimes be quite rapid – unchanging cultures are dead ones! However, no human society and no human beings are ever without culture. It is a constant and absolutely fundamental feature of all existence wherever people are found.

Although culture takes many visible forms – for example, in the customs that people practise and the things that they produce – in its essence it is a thing of the mind. In this sense, it is like an invisible map that everybody within a society retains in their minds, and which gives guidance to them. It is the mental plan by which they organize themselves as a society and are able to live in their environment. At the very deepest level, it moulds the way in which they understand the nature and meaning of the world around them, and it is this profound level of culture that is known as worldview. Worldview is the way in which people who belong to a particular culture make sense of the world they live in and how it works, and of their own place and role in it – their lives and experiences.

---

[2]L. Luzbetak, *Church and Cultures* (New York: Orbis, 1988), 156.

Worldview is thus the shared understanding of reality – of truth – held by a particular society.

It is at the level of worldview that religion has a profound impact on culture. The religion that a community holds shapes the way in which they understand reality – their worldview. This is necessarily so because worldview sets out to answer the biggest and most important questions that men and women can ask, such as - who are we? Where do we come from? Why are we here? Where are we going? How should we behave? What is time? Why do we suffer? What other beings exist? What are they like? The answers to such questions invariably emerge, at least in part, from the beliefs of a particular religion and, taken together, they create the worldview. So, although worldview is invisible in the sense that it exists primarily in human minds, it nevertheless takes visible form in the ways in which people behave, as their acts and customs give concrete expression to their beliefs. For example, if people believe that suffering may be caused by sorcerers who have hidden power to harm them, they will take measures to protect themselves against sorcery – perhaps by trying to identify the sorcerers and punishing them, or by wearing charms and fetishes intended to shield themselves or their property from the sorcerers' powers. Those who do not believe in sorcery will not behave in these ways. In the West, therefore, instead of using fetishes people might try to protect themselves from illness and misfortune by taking vitamin supplements and making sure their insurance policies are up-to-date, an approach which reflects a more materialistic worldview. As this example shows, careful and patient observation of people's behaviour can help us to determine their worldview.

Worldview is particularly tenacious. People do not easily or quickly abandon beliefs and moral values which their parents have passed down to them, which everybody else in their society also holds, and which define for them the nature of reality and so make sense of their experience. A people's own culture and worldview seem natural and self-evident to them, and under normal circumstances are simply unquestionable. Nevertheless, there are situations in which a people may begin to question their worldview assumptions. For example, when cultures encounter one another, and a people is confronted with ideas quite different from their own, worldview beliefs may be challenged and change may result. More profoundly, catastrophic situations such as war or famine may arise, in which a people finds that the beliefs that explained reality to them and sustained them in the past are no longer able to perform those functions. However, normally people are simply unaware of having particular worldview beliefs: the idea that there could be some other understanding of the world is quite foreign to them, and even absurd.

The tenacity of worldview – its resistance to change – is evident when people respond to the gospel of Jesus Christ while continuing to hold worldview beliefs that conflict with it. For example, in recent decades huge numbers of African people have embraced the Christian faith and no longer adhere outwardly to the religions of their forefathers. Nevertheless, their traditional worldview – which has been substantially shaped by African traditional religion – continues powerfully to shape their beliefs and lives. As a result, many professing Christians may hold beliefs and behave in ways which are incompatible with the Christian truth that they have outwardly embraced. In consequence, their Christian faith may seem at times to be little more than a veneer that has been glued over the surface of their lives, while underneath nothing much has altered: the gospel of Christ has not penetrated the depths of worldview and so lives are relatively unchanged.

Nor is this just a feature of African Christianity; it is true all over the world. The secular and materialistic worldview prevalent in western countries may similarly impact the lives of European and American Christians. In consequence, although they have confessed Jesus Christ, in great measure their beliefs, attitudes, ambitions and behaviour may be scarcely, if at all, different from those of their non-Christian neighbours. Whenever this happens the result is syncretism, which can be defined as the mixing of the gospel with major elements drawn from a non-Christian worldview, whose tendency is to compromise the integrity of the Christian faith that is outwardly professed.

We can see the same tendency evident among the believers and churches that we encounter in the New Testament. For example, the Greeks would have rejected the notion of the resurrection of human bodies as they regarded the body as a prison of the soul; for them, therefore, death was the soul's liberation from that prison. Hence Paul had to write at length to believers in the church at Corinth in order to prove and explain the Christian doctrine of resurrection (1 Cor. 15). He was seeking to transform a deeply held worldview belief – one that seemed to be obviously true to his readers, and which they therefore clung on to resolutely even though they had accepted the gospel.

In more general terms, Paul urged the Roman Christians, "be transformed by the renewing of your mind" (Rom. 12:1). Those he was writing to in Rome had put their faith in Christ and were seeking to live as Christians. Paul recognised, however, that if their new-found faith was to be a reality in every area of their lives, then their minds – their thinking – needed to be changed at the deepest level; for what people *think* – the worldview that they hold – determines what they are and the way in which they live: *we are what we think*. True Christian discipleship therefore demands that worldview be thoroughly sifted in the light of the gospel, and be transformed by it. What makes this immensely difficult to achieve is the fact that worldview beliefs are so very deeply rooted in human thinking, and seem so patently true and inevitable to those who hold them. However, if Christian believers are to grow in their faith, then worldview change is essential; without it people may call themselves Christians but their lives will continue to be controlled by their pre-Christian beliefs.

The purpose of the following chapters is to examine one particularly significant aspect of the traditional African worldview – belief in a world of sorcerers and unseen spirits – in the light of the gospel, with a view to the transformation of belief and life. Two points need to be made. First, biblical teaching alone is the criterion by which the beliefs of any worldview may be assessed and corrected, and not the contrasting worldview of another culture. In other words, the objective here is not to reshape the African worldview in order to bring it into conformity with that of the West or of any other culture; rather, it is to evaluate and transform it by submitting it to the judgement of the word of God. All human cultures are imperfect and in need of transformation; none is able to stand in judgement on another.

Second, the issue of traditional African beliefs in the invisible world has been neglected in the past, as if the gospel had nothing to say about it. Part of the reason for this is that in the nineteenth and twentieth centuries the good news of Jesus Christ was brought to Africa largely by western missionaries. In many cases, their worldview no longer had much place for the notion of sorcerers, and very little place for spirits either, despite abundant biblical testimony to their existence.

Consequently, they had given little – if any – thought to these matters, even though they are of central importance in African conceptions of reality. They had no biblical responses to the pressing questions of their new converts, because they had never had to face those questions in their own experience: can a Christian be injured – even killed – by a witch, or harmed by the curse and the evil eye, or afflicted and possessed by a spirit? Should believers continue to revere and care for their deceased ancestors? Do the ancestors still contact them in dreams – indeed, did they ever do so? Is it acceptable to get in touch with the invisible world in pursuit of solutions to illness, drought and barrenness?

> When tribal people spoke of fear of evil spirits, [western missionaries] denied the existence of the spirits rather than claim the power of Christ over them.[3]

---

[3]P.G. Hiebert, *Anthropological Reflections on Missiological Issues* (Grand Rapids: Baker, 1994), 197.

This was a serious failure in the effective discipling of new believers. Too often, it left them with the impression that the gospel had nothing to say about the invisible world and the menace it represented – apart from a prohibition of all contact with it. Therefore, feeling the need for protection, they continued to deal with the threat that it posed in the old traditional ways.

To summarise, failure to address the issue of witches and spirits from a solidly Christian perspective left a whole area of life unredeemed – excluded from the saving power of the gospel, so that new believers felt obliged to use the remedies they had trusted in before they came to know Christ. However, if believers of any culture are to follow Christ in faithful discipleship, then every aspect of their lives must come under his lordship. The alternative is a faith crippled by syncretism.

Questions for further reflection

1. How should a Christian regard his or her own culture?

2. In what areas did Jesus challenge the culture of his time? How did he do it?

3. What areas of worldview in your culture are in need of transformation?

4. Is there a biblical worldview?

5. Identify some of the cultural challenges likely to be encountered when missionaries enter a culture other than their own with the good news.

CHAPTER 2

THE AFRICAN WORLDVIEW

There is a belief in Gikuyu that illness is carried to the people by some kind of evil spirits. These are believed to conceal themselves in the bushes around the homesteads, and when they want to launch a mass attack on the people they are carried by winds from one homestead to another. On these occasions the evil spirits are said to travel during the day. When a whirlwind is seen in its terrific speed, one can hear people shouting and abusing vigorously what is believed to be the mass of evil spirits gathering their forces for general attack on the people.

On the outbreak of an epidemic or illness, the cause of which people cannot clearly understand nor find any effective remedies in their wide range of herbal treatments, the elders of various grades meet to consult seers and diviners to find out how they can relieve the people from their suffering. In this consultation it is reported that medical aid has failed and that physical force has to be applied against the enemy. It is then decided that the only way to get rid of such a malady is to prepare a real fight with the evil spirits which have so unkindly brought suffering upon the community. For it is believed that if the evil spirits are defeated in battle, not only will they run away and take with them the illness, but also that they will be frightened and it will be unlikely that they will in future dare to bring misery to the people.

It is ritually considered that the evening is the best time to wage war against the evil spirits. They are then believed to be round about near the unfortunate homesteads, so as to be able to make records of their victims. After consultation of the elders, the day is decided upon on the evening of which the fight will start against the unseen creatures. The most favourable moment for the ritual fight is when the moon comes out, about seven o'clock in the evening. Following the elders' decision, notices are sent out by word of mouth announcing the date of the battle. The news is carried out from homestead to homestead, from village to village, and from district to district. In this way the people are told to prepare themselves for the ritual fight and to be in readiness for the signal. The custom in respect to this ceremony requires that all members of the community, old and young, should participate ceremonially in the battle.

On the evening appointed, war horns . . . are sounded from various centres to signal the starting of the battle against the malicious spirits. On hearing the war horns, men, women, and children, armed with stocks, clubs, and other weapons, rush from their huts in great excitement. The elders take great care to see that spears, swords, and knives are not used in this fight, for it is feared that if the spirits' blood is shed on the land its uncleanliness might spread defilement which might cause great calamity in the community. To avoid misery and suffering people are asked to use only blunt weapons.

As soon as the people are ready they come out of their homesteads and form ceremonial fighting units. They start beating their sticks together in the rhythm characteristic of this ritual, and

*at the same time they shout and scream furiously, moving slowly
towards the river. On the way down they beat bushes along the side
of the paths, and examine them carefully to make sure that they
do not leave behind any malicious spirit hiding in these bushes.*[1]

Historically each African people has tended to have its
own distinctive religion. This has stirred some debate as
to whether one should speak of African traditional *religion*
or of African traditional *religions*. Certainly there is a good
deal of diversity among them. However, at the same time
common themes recur which make it possible to speak of
an African worldview, which despite variation, pervades sub-
Saharan Africa to a large extent. Indeed, many of the themes
of African religion discussed here can be found in other
so-called 'primal' religions throughout the world. They also
persist in the popular 'folk' religious forms of the great world
religions such as Islam and Hinduism, as well as in syncretistic
expressions of Christianity. Consequently, the relevance of
what is said here and in the following chapters is not limited
to the worldview of traditional Africa, but has a much broader
significance.

Central features of the African Worldview

Many observers, both Africans and others, have identified
central features of such a worldview. First, it has
a strongly communal emphasis, in contrast with
the individualism typical of modern western cultures.

---

[1] J. Kenyatta, *Facing Mount Kenya* (London & Nairobi: Heinemann, 1979),
260-262. Reproduced by permission of East African Educational Publishers
Ltd., Nairobi, Kenya.

Interpersonal relationships are given the highest priority and
a person's identity is rooted in their membership of a group
rather than in their own existence as an independent human
being. In the words of John Mbiti, in African thinking, "I am,
because we are; and since we are, therefore, I am."[2] Second,
traditional African thinking is holistic, and does not divide life
into sacred and secular areas. Equally, there is no separation
between visible and invisible worlds because together they
make up an indivisible unity, one single reality. This is
illustrated by the fact that for most peoples there is no word
for religion; consciousness of the spiritual realm impacts and
permeates the whole of life and is not confined to a specifically
'religious' area. One result of this sort of thinking is that
'secular' activities like hunting, travelling or farming may all
have a 'religious' dimension; for example, before cultivating
the land a farmer may offer a sacrifice to a spirit such as
an earth goddess. In a similar way suffering is understood
not just as a physical problem but a spiritual one too. Third,
the world is seen as good, and something to be enjoyed.
Asceticism, expressed for example in a high view of celibacy
(which has been very influential in the western tradition), is
generally quite alien to African thought. There is optimism
about life, but awareness too that it is unpredictable and that
the harmony and benevolence, which should exist, are always
fragile. The arrival of suffering indicates that at some point the
delicate balance has been upset. There is also a utilitarian and
pragmatic approach to the spiritual dimension of life. People
occupy themselves with 'religious' ritual in order to ensure
the continued fertility of fields, animals and wives, to keep

---

[2]J. Mbiti, *African Religions and Philosophy* (Oxford: Heinemann, 1969), 105.

themselves free from illness, accident and whatever other misfortunes might afflict them, and to maintain harmony among themselves.

Finally – and for present purposes the most important aspect of the African worldview – there is a distinctive approach towards suffering. This is concisely expressed in a Zulu proverb, 'There is always somebody.' In traditional thinking, affliction invariably occurs because some personal agent has brought it about. The culprit might be God himself, but more usually it will be identified as a spirit or as a human being operating through witchcraft or sorcery. Anger alone may be seen as a force powerful enough to reach out and harm another person. Accordingly, there is no such thing as an accident. If a fisherman drowns when his dugout capsizes, if a farmer is struck by lightning, or if a traveller is bitten by a snake – in all such cases somebody is responsible. The same is true of illness, and even death demands an explanation in such terms, except perhaps in the case of the very old.

However, the pursuit of personal explanation for cases of suffering does not necessarily mean ignorance of their obvious physical causes. People know that hippopotamuses upset dugout canoes, that lightning strikes and that snakebites kill. With the arrival of modern medical science, they are also well aware of the role of germs and viruses in causing illness. However, the traditional personal explanation seeks to go beyond the purely physical causes of an event to the underlying reasons for it: it goes beyond the question of 'how' an event occurred and attempts to answer the question 'why?' For example, many people may have travelled along a particular path over many years, but why did the snake appear at this time to bite this particular person? Mosquitoes may carry the malaria parasite, but why did this particular person die of it and not the many other people also bitten by the same mosquito? In the western worldview the search for meaning at this level has largely been abandoned: a person dies in a car crash because they just happened to be in the wrong place at the wrong time – it was bad luck. African peoples have not been satisfied with explanations of this sort, which would leave them, as they leave westerners, in an ultimately meaningless and inexplicable cosmos.

As they look for the meaning of their sufferings, African peoples seek the services of a specialist to help them – the 'diviner'. The role of diviner has tended to be one of the most influential and prestigious in society, for it is he or she who is supposed to be able to penetrate the unseen world of spirits and occult power and 'see' what is taking place there, who is doing what to whom. Therefore, afflicted people and their families turn to the diviner to identify the particular cause of a given affliction and prescribe the appropriate remedy. As a diviner said,

> People come to me to find out what is causing their problems. It is my work to divine the cause of the evil, to figure out the source of the immorality that is provoking the problem. Once the immorality is identified then the person can take steps to neutralize it.[3]

Diviners use a variety of techniques to penetrate the world of sorcerers and invisible spirits, including devices such as

---

[3]M. C. Kirwen, *The Missionary and the Diviner* (Maryknoll: Orbis, 1987), 29.

the casting of stones or shells, possession by a spirit familiar, or the sacrifice of animals, as well as careful questioning of the enquirer. Nevertheless, whatever the procedure they use, divination is the central moment in responding to any incident of misfortune. It looks back to the cause and forward to the remedy. The diviner is therefore the most important human link with the invisible world.

God and spirits

African peoples have traditionally been profoundly religious. Belief in a supreme being, the creator of the world, is almost universal, although for many peoples he is a God who has largely withdrawn from the world he made. The notion of his separation from his creation is expressed in numerous myths found right across the continent, some of which speak of an act of human wrongdoing that brought about his withdrawal. There is a widespread feeling that God is so great that he cannot really be concerned with the mundane lives of ordinary men and women, although some peoples do try to come before him, and prayers may be offered to him. Nevertheless, God's 'absence' has several important implications for the African worldview.

It means that the world of lesser spirits and spiritual forces takes on much greater importance than might be the case if God was close at hand and active in the world. From a religious perspective, that spiritual world becomes the focus of human attention. God's absence also means there is nothing that can bring order to the invisible realm, which is therefore just a chaos of competing powers. This in turn brings a strong sense of danger to human beings who feel a constant threat from the invisible and uncontrolled powers around them, and who seek to negotiate with these powers to avert disaster. In addition, in traditional thought the invisible world is morally ambiguous. Although there are some exceptions, for most peoples there is no clear-cut distinction between angelic and demonic spirits. Angels and demons are distinguished in the Bible in terms of their relationship with the creator: angels are beings which serve him while demons are those that rebel against him.

However, in the African conception, since God is absent, spirits are evaluated in terms of their relationship with human beings. So, they may bring trouble and so be 'demonic', but by using the right approach people tend to believe that they can also be pacified and even become sources of 'blessing'.

The world of spirits, including the spirits of deceased ancestors, is richly populated. Some peoples believe in particularly powerful spirits, which are often referred to as divinities. These may be associated with natural phenomena like the rain or harvest, or with certain illnesses like smallpox, or they may be linked with a particular clan - some peoples see them as the spirits of the founders of the clan, or even of the tribe. Among the Sudanese Dinka 'clan-divinities', for example, are spirits of descent groups, and the Nyoro of Uganda revere the bacwezi spirits as founders of their ruling dynasty. Nevertheless, many peoples do not recognize divinities, but ancestor veneration is extremely widespread and very important. It is, in some respects, an extension of the way society operates among the living. As people increase in age, they gain respect and authority as elders of their family, clan or tribe. At death they do not cease to belong to their families but increase further in status: they are the 'living dead', no longer visible but still present and powerfully influential in the lives of their descendants. At this stage the veneration offered to them comes very close to worship. The ancestors should not be seen simply as mediators between their living descendants and God himself: veneration is addressed to the ancestors as ancestors, because it is they who are able to give life and plenty – or to bring disaster – to their descendants.

People believe that ancestors continue to communicate with the living in order to guide, warn, and punish. Communication may take place through dreams, but more importantly it is supposed to happen through the sufferings that ancestors supposedly inflict for various reasons. Accordingly, people suppose that ancestors afflict their living kin when they do not receive the respect they deserve, or when the living cease to follow the traditions that the ancestors established in the past, or when there is disharmony within the community. For some peoples ancestor veneration has also been a major element in preserving ethnic identity through times of crisis. On the other hand, the living themselves sustain the ancestors by remembering their names and making offerings to them. As their names are forgotten, they cease to be 'living dead' and enter a state of collective immortality: their continued individual existence is lost and they can no longer intervene in the lives of their descendants.

While ancestors bring blessing and represent the ideals of a people, their presence can also be threatening. Attitudes vary from one people to another, but certainly for many they are felt as a constant menace. From the perspective of their living descendants, offerings made to them have a double meaning: on the one hand, they express hospitality, but they are also requests to the 'living dead' to keep a distance. This is true also of funeral rites, which aim not only to integrate the deceased back into the community in their new role as ancestors, but also to make sure that they keep a healthy distance from it.

There are many other spirits in traditional African belief. There are the spirits of human beings who are not integrated into the ancestor cult. This may be because they received no proper burial, or they died away from home, or they were identified as witches. There are spirits of dead animals, and hunters may sometimes offer a sacrifice to the spirit of an animal they have killed to ensure that it does not subsequently attack them. Mandari believe in vengeful nyok, which are the spirits of animals slain by humans, of deformed babies exposed to die, and of homicide victims. Some spirits were created as such and may be associated with particular natural phenomena – a waterfall, a mountain, an outcrop of rock, a tree – or may simply wander unattached to a special place. Spirits may also be linked with a piece of agricultural land and have to be placated before cultivation can begin. There are spirits that cause diseases and some that possess and empower witches. The Shona believe witches are possessed by the spirit of the hyena which, supposedly like the witch, hunts by night and eats dead meat.

Human beings and the spirit world

Human beings venerate spirits, including those of the ancestors. Very often the connection with a spirit has been passed down through generations, especially in the case of the ancestors, but sometimes a new relationship may be initiated. Humans may themselves try to forge a bond with a spirit previously unknown to them, but more frequently new relationships are established when a spirit 'attacks' a human being. Spirit 'attack' can take many forms, and the identification of what really constitutes such an attack depends on criteria that vary greatly from one people to another. Most often it is experienced as an illness, which for some peoples may take a purely physical form, while for others it might include 'possession' of the victim by the spirit. This may be evidenced by mental disorder and bizarre behaviour including flights into the bush, frenzied periods of activity, nakedness, extraordinary feats of strength or endurance, and uncontrollability. However, for some peoples the evidence that a spirit has entered somebody and 'possessed' them may take the form of physical symptoms alone, such as headache or fever. There are also those who believe that different spirits attack in different ways, and the victim's symptoms indicate the exact identity of the spirit concerned. In any given society, it is the role of the diviner to interpret the meaning of the illness and, if caused by a spirit, to establish its identity and prescribe the appropriate remedy.

The response to spirit attack depends on the culture concerned and the exact diagnosis provided by the diviner. In broad terms there are three possible approaches. First, there is appeasement, which means acknowledging and satisfying the supposed grievances of the spirit. Typically, this takes place when ancestors are identified as the source of the problem, and will likely take the form of sacrifice and invocations, such as this one by the Mende:

Ah, grandfathers, I have come to you: Momo is the
one who is ill. The soothsayer informs me that you are
angry with him because he has not 'fed' you for a long
time. Do you, grandfathers, kindly pardon him. He is
a small boy; he has no senses yet. I have come now to
beg you. My heart is now clear.[4]

Among the Mandari of Sudan some illnesses are caused by
spirits called *jok*. They are placated by an initial sacrifice and
the setting up of a shrine, followed by regularly 'feeding' the
spirit in the form of sacrifice and libation. It then becomes the
protector of the family in question.

A second response is exorcism, which simply means
expelling the spirit and terminating all relationship with
it, although some satisfaction of its demands may also be
required. Exorcism is the response employed when the spirit
is seen as purely evil or unknown. Accommodation is the
third response and resembles appeasement, except that the
victim must be 'possessed' by the spirit as part of the cure.
The spirit will be encouraged to enter and take control of its
prey, and then to state the terms under which the affliction
will cease. Among those terms, it may well demand that it be
allowed to re-possess the person concerned on a regular basis.
In this way, accommodation may open up the possibility of
a new role for the victim, perhaps as a shaman – a master
of spirits who is able to diagnose and cure the afflictions of
others, or as a medium – the mouthpiece of the spirit who can
operate as a diviner. Either role may bring rich social prestige
as well as material rewards. Alternatively, accommodation

[4]K. Little, 'The Mende in Sierra Leone', in D. Forde (ed.), *African Worlds*
(London: Oxford University Press, 1954), 117.

may lead to membership of a spirit possession cult, whose members – mainly women – meet periodically to experience ecstatic trance. Such cults have been widespread across much of Africa.

Witchcraft and sorcery

Belief in witchcraft has existed in almost every culture throughout the course of history and, although the exact content of witchcraft beliefs varies from one culture to another, it is widespread and deep-seated in African tradition. Underlying all such beliefs is the idea that human beings are able to harm one another by occult, mystical, non-physical means. Anger alone may hurt another person, especially within certain relationships or if the victim is in what is regarded as a mystically dangerous state – perhaps going through a rite of initiation, for example. Many peoples believe in the power of the curse, which may be employed in anger, or by an elder to punish unacceptable behaviour.

Witchcraft beliefs can be quite complex. Sometimes a distinction is made between witchcraft and sorcery. Witchcraft is then understood as the ability to harm another person by means of an innate power that some people possess, perhaps because of a special substance in their bodies or from a relationship with a spirit. Those believed to possess the 'evil eye' might also fall within this category. Sorcery, on the other hand, involves the use of material objects, incantations and ritual activity to harm another person. In principle it might be used by anybody who knows the appropriate techniques.

The distinction between witchcraft and sorcery is a useful one, but cannot be simply applied to all African peoples, some of whom have rather more complex belief systems. The Lugbara, for example, have traditionally believed in six different types of mystic evildoer. Nor are witchcraft and sorcery used simply for causing harm to others. Witchcraft may also be seen as a means of self-advancement, although even in such cases it is still frequently activated through some socially unacceptable act such as incest. As societies have experienced 'modernisation' in the post-colonial era, witchcraft may often be seen as the path to new forms of wealth or political power, to sporting or sexual success, and so on. In these circumstances, it is viewed with ambivalence: it remains no doubt a terrifying and evil thing, but equally one that has much to offer. Sorcery too slides into the use of acceptable 'medicine' to protect oneself *against* attack, or to ensure the fertility of one's herds or fields.

Recently there has also been significant change in the profile of witchcraft suspects. Traditionally witches tended to be women, and more often elderly women. Those accused were unsocial, solitary and childless; they may have been eccentric, or had some physical disability or deformity. Ethnic minorities were also more vulnerable to accusation. In brief, those who did not conform to society's norms and expectations were more likely to be scapegoated as witches. However, in recent years there has been a quite new and growing tendency for children to be accused of witchcraft. This phenomenon can be variously explained, but it probably reflects social and economic changes taking place across much of Africa: an increase in individualism, the often early financial independence of children, the weakening of family structures, the upsurge of vulnerable and unwanted orphans due to AIDS, war and general social dislocation, and the phenomenon of child soldiers.[5]

The power of witchcraft and sorcery belief lies to a large extent in its ability to explain misfortune. However, such beliefs also enable people to evade personal responsibility for failure. In this way witchcraft beliefs sustain a worldview of fatalism and passivity. Accordingly, the success of a neighbour, and one's own failure, can be attributed to witchcraft, as can illness, death and accidental injury. Some peoples explain almost every misfortune of whatever nature in terms of witchcraft, as seems to have been the case among the Azande of Sudan:

> If blight seizes the ground-nut crop it is witchcraft; if the bush is vainly scoured for game it is witchcraft; if women laboriously bale water out of a pool and are rewarded by but a few fish it is witchcraft; if termites do not rise when their swarming is due and a cold useless night is spent waiting for their flight it is witchcraft; if a wife is sulky and unresponsive to her husband it is witchcraft; if a prince is cold and distant with his subject it is witchcraft; if, in fact, any failure or misfortune falls upon anybody at any time and in relation to any of the manifold activities of his life it may be due to witchcraft.[6]

Inevitably, individuals and whole societies make efforts to protect themselves against the power of the witch. At the simplest level this means the use of charms to ward off the

---

[5]A. Cimpric, *Children Accused of Witchcraft: An anthropological study of contemporary practices in Africa*, (Dakar: UNICEF, 2010), 20-24.
[6]E. E. Evans-Pritchard, *Witchcraft, Oracles and Magic among the Azande* (Oxford: Clarendon Press, 1976 [1937]), 18.

evil that the witch or sorcerer might initiate. Such charms may be worn by an individual, buried in the floor or roof of a house, or hidden in the corner of a field. Sometimes the charms are believed to cause the intended evil to rebound on the witch or sorcerer. Various methods are also used to detect witches when people believe that they have been active in causing some affliction. Sometimes this involves a rite – perhaps the slaughter of a chicken and close observation of the way in which it dies – which will indicate the guilty party; alternatively there are peoples who use ordeals in which suspected witches must plunge their hand into boiling water or swallow poison. The Zande people remove a supposed victim of witchcraft to the bush, where he or she will be hidden from the evil attention of the unknown witch. Meanwhile they launch special 'medicine' against the witch, withdrawing it only when their oracles show that the guilty party has succumbed.

Among some peoples there is the specialist role of witch-finder, some of whom are believed to have the power to 'smell' witchcraft. There are guilds whose members work together to root out witches, such as the Nupe ndako gboya, or Yoruba oro societies. At various times in the twentieth century, there have also been witch-cleansing movements, such as the Bamucapi movement in Central Africa. These have sometimes covered large areas of the continent, and supposedly cleansed them systematically of all witches. Churches have adopted rather similar approaches; among the Aladura in West Africa it was believed that witches had to confess if they drank specially sanctified 'holy water'. Indeed, in recent years the supposed ability of some churches to identify witches and exorcise

them of their witchcraft powers, has enabled them to attract
adherents gripped by fear of witches.

> Church growth is directly linked to that fear. People
> seek protection from witches and thus help fuel
> the unprecedented growth of Christianity in Africa.
> Many, from top government officials to the lowest in
> society, join neo-Pentecostal churches because of their
> emphasis on deliverance and protection.[7]

Some churches apparently have a vested interest in
maintaining witchcraft fears.

Finally, there is the simple witch-hunt, which can occur
when witchcraft paranoia grips a society. This may involve the
indiscriminate accusation of neighbours followed by summary
justice (or injustice) meted out on those found guilty.
However, whatever measures are employed to eliminate
witchcraft and sorcery, people continue to suffer and die:
accordingly, in the logic of witchcraft belief, the witch is never
eliminated.

Conclusion

Within the traditional African worldview, beliefs in spirits and
sorcerers have been used to explain the coming of misfortune
and so enable victims to respond, both by indicating potential
sources of suffering and by providing appropriate strategies of
response. Such beliefs deal with one of the biggest questions
with which any worldview must grapple – that of suffering –
and one that is of central importance in the African context.

---

[7]S. Agang, 'Who's Afraid of Witches', in *Christianity Today*
(September 2009) at http://www.christianitytoday.com/ct/2009/
septemberweb-only/137-21.0.html

At the same time, they leave human beings in a universe that is constantly threatening. In fact, in the case of witchcraft, they may actually produce reactions that aggravate human suffering rather than alleviating it, by creating an atmosphere of fear, suspicion and vengeance among neighbours and even close family members. Nor do the solutions proposed ever produce a final and definitive answer to the problems they are meant to resolve.

Questions for further reflection

1. Is there always somebody?

2. From a biblical perspective, is the pursuit of meaning in affliction legitimate?

3. What might be the principal elements of a Christian 'theology of the ancestors'?

4. How effectively do traditional African cultures cope with the problem of spirit-caused affliction?

5. Are people right to fear witches and sorcerers?

CHAPTER 3

~~~

THE BIBLE AND THE UNSEEN WORLD

I venture to assert that what we are about to consider is more relevant to the condition of the world than all talk about politics and international relationships and everything in which statesmen and their followers indulge. That is a strong and bold statement, as I am well aware; but if you believe the Bible at all, it must inevitably be true. We are dealing, remember, with the ultimate cause of the world situation, and for this reason I can say that this is more urgently relevant than anything else. Let me use a comparison which I have often employed. It seems to me that what modern thinkers so constantly fail to do is to differentiate between a disease itself and the possible symptoms of a disease. A disease may give rise to many symptoms. Take any example at random. With influenza prevalent you may get pneumonia. The primary disease is, in a sense, in your lungs. Let that do for the moment as a rough definition of pneumonia. But you will find that you have many symptoms. You will have a headache, you will feel flushed, you may have odd aches and pains all over your body, and there may be sweating and so on. There are very many symptoms of the disease, and the danger is that we should spend our time in medicating the symptoms only. You can take various

things to relieve your headache, such as aspirin, and your head
will feel better for a while. But it will not make any difference to
the pneumonia. And so you can go on dealing with one thing after
another. You will find that you are kept very busy, and that you
will have to go on dealing with fresh symptoms constantly. But
the disease itself, and not the symptoms, is the thing that really
matters.

What is the chief problem with the world at this moment?
Here are all the statesmen and others meeting busily in conference,
quarrelling, breaking up, and then meeting again. What is the
matter? The problem is that they do not realize the nature of the
disease, and they have not understood the cause. ...

The business of the church is to get down to the root cause
of the trouble. It alone can do so. And it is because what we are
looking at here gives the only true understanding of the world
situation and what can be done about it, that I am claiming for it
that it is the most urgently relevant message in this troubled world
of ours today.

First of all the Apostle directs us to the fact of the conflict.
You notice his terms, 'We wrestle.' ... We are participators in this
mighty spiritual conflict that is going on round and about us and
in us. But we are also individually engaged, every one of us. [1]

In significant respects, the traditional African worldview
resembles the picture of reality that emerges from the Old
and New Testaments. The Bible stresses human community
and solidarity, while not losing sight of the importance of

---

[1]D. M. Lloyd-Jones, *The Christian Warfare: An Exposition of Ephesians 6:10*
to 13 (Edinburgh: The Banner of Truth Trust, 1976), 39-40. Reproduced by
permission of The Banner of Truth Trust, Edinburgh, U.K.

the individual person. It is also profoundly affirming of the created world, which is good because God made it and pronounced it to be good. Consequently, it is also holistic, for everything that exists has been made by God and is subject to him, and human beings may seek his glory in all the dimensions of life. The Bible also affirms the existence of an invisible spiritual realm, populated by an immense variety of divinely created spirit beings who influence what happens on earth. Nevertheless, at some extremely important points the biblical vision of reality parts company with the African worldview, and the similarities must not blind us to the great differences. It is the purpose of this chapter to bring the biblical perspective into focus, and allow it to evaluate African conceptions of the invisible world and its significance for human beings.

God and creation

The doctrine of creation is fundamental to all Christian theology. It means not only that God created the world, both visible and invisible, but also that he continues to be intimately involved with it – indeed to sustain it moment by moment (Col. 1:17; Heb. 1:3). In contrast with the remote God widely found in African traditional religion, the God of the Bible is emphatically present throughout the cosmos he has made, and he rules over all of it: he is both immanent and sovereign.

This in turn has two important implications. First, in the Bible the spiritual domain is not characterized by the sort of moral ambiguity that is widespread within the African worldview. The moral status of invisible beings – as of human beings – is determined by their relationship with God himself. Those that have remained faithful to him are unambiguously good, and those that have rebelled are unmitigatedly evil. The Bible makes the distinction between them very clear. Second, the whole of the spiritual world is under God's sovereign rule, including the rebellious spirits. It is not a lawless chaos, as it is in African tradition. God created all spirits and all are infinitely inferior to him. This means that while he allows some spirits to continue in their rebellion, he nevertheless determines and limits what they may and may not do, and ultimately uses them and their acts for his own purposes. This is clear, for example, when Satan asks God whether he may test Job or Peter (Job 1-2; Luke 22:31-32).

Any attempt to understand the biblical vision of the unseen world must begin with a clear grasp of the sovereign creator God and his universal reign, which puts spirits – powerful as they might be – in clear perspective.

Satan and the kingdom of darkness

The biblical figure of Satan has few parallels in African religions, although one or two peoples come close to recognising the existence of a spirit of total evil. umTyholi among the Xhosa, for example, is creator of evil things, and the Dinka divinity Macardit is the ultimate explanation for all suffering and evil. Such beings, however, are rare. In the Bible, Satan, the devil, is a creature. He owes his creation and his continuing existence to God, in the same way that rebellious men and women do. Like all that God made, he was created good, and he was one of the company of angels. This means that he is a spirit without physical substance, but also a person with intelligence, will, self-consciousness and the ability to engage in personal relationships through speech. In other words, he is not simply an impersonal force like the wind or electricity.

Given that Satan was created good but is now evil, it is clear that at some point he must have fallen from a state of perfection by his own act of deliberate, conscious rebellion —indeed the very name, Satan, means 'adversary'. The Bible says little of the moment of his rebellion, but Jesus suggests his fall when he says that he did not stand in the truth (John 8:44), which implies that once he was in the truth but did not stay there. Again, in Revelation John uses a vivid image to indicate that he led a significant number of his fellow angels in rebellion with himself (12:4). Certain prophetic passages of the Old Testament have also been seen as allusions to Satan's fall, especially Isaiah 14:12-20 and Ezekiel 28:12-19. However, in the Isaiah text the prophet is speaking of Babylon, and in Ezekiel of Tyre. In neither passage is there a specific reference to Satan. It is, therefore, doubtful whether one can use them to explain the origin of Satan and of evil.

From all that the Bible teaches about angels, Satan is, without doubt, vastly more powerful than humans; he has far greater intelligence; and he can move rapidly around the earth (Job 1:7; 2:2). However, he is infinitely inferior to God: despite his great power, his immense knowledge and his capacity for rapid movement, he does not possess the divine attributes of omnipotence, omniscience and omnipresence. Nor is he a self-existent, creative source of life, which uniquely belongs to the triune God: "as the Father has life in himself, so he has granted the Son to have life in himself" (John 5:26).

It is vital to understand this. Any approach to Satan and the forces of darkness that puts them on a level of equality with God, and so puts the outcome of God's final victory over them in doubt, is quite contrary to the teaching of Scripture. Satan is not another god – he is not an evil god; he is indeed evil but infinitely inferior to his creator and subject to him. When Paul describes him as the "god of this world" (2 Cor. 4:4) the expression refers to the fact that consciously or, more likely, unconsciously, unredeemed people are under Satan's control and do his will. Satan seeks to usurp God's place by enslaving fallen humanity to his own will. All of this means that as he fights against God's eternal purposes he is, and always has been, doomed: he struggles and rages against God but with no hope at all. His rebellion is, therefore, finally futile, meaning that evil itself is ultimately futile and meaningless.

Satan exercises power over a realm of fallen spirits who are also in rebellion against God. This demonic world is a kingdom, quite unlike the anarchy of African spirits. The Bible uses numerous terms to refer to these fallen spirits, but it nowhere offers a systematic description of their different ranks and identities, nor does it indicate their numbers or locations. The reality and general nature of the realm of darkness are revealed, but the details are not, perhaps an implicit warning on the part of the writers of Scripture that these are areas not to be pried into. Indeed, speculation about such matters beyond what the Bible reveals suggests an unwholesome preoccupation with the powers of evil and the enemies of God rather than with God himself.

Demons or unclean spirits are encountered mostly in the gospels and Acts, where their main activity is to cause physical illness and to 'possess' people, a phenomenon which will be discussed later. Like Satan, they have characteristics of personality including will and intelligence, and are not just evil forces. For instance, they speak to Jesus, know who he is, and try to resist him. Satan's rule over them is made clear when Jesus responds to his adversaries' accusation that he expelled demons by the power of Beelzebub: "How can Satan drive out Satan? . . . if Satan is divided and opposes himself he cannot stand" (Mark 3:23). He is saying that the demons who afflicted possessed people were doing so as agents of Satan under his direction – they were members of the kingdom of darkness over which Satan ruled.

In some of Paul's letters and in 1 Peter there are references to *rulers, authorities, powers* and *dominions*, which are invariably to be understood as spirits of a demonic nature (Rom. 8:38; 1 Cor. 15:24-25; Eph. 1:21; 3:10; 6:12; Col. 1:16; 2:10,15; 1 Pet. 3:22). Thus in Ephesians 6:12 it is against these beings that Christians must struggle, while in Colossians 2:15 they are clearly enemies whom Christ has disarmed, having triumphed over them. The beings identified as rulers, authorities and so on may well be the same as those called demons or unclean spirits in the gospels, although it is possible that demonic beings of a higher order are at times in view. Finally, while the Bible usually uses the term angel to refer to spirits who faithfully serve God, occasionally it is also used to refer to those that are rebellious, and who are sometimes explicitly identified as angels of Satan himself (Matt. 25:41; 2 Pet. 2:4; Jude 1:6; Rev. 12:7,9).

Satan also exercises power over fallen humanity, which the New Testament mentions on numerous occasions. Jesus describes Satan as "the prince of this world" three times (John 12:31; 14:30; 16:11). As we have noticed, Paul refers to him as the "god of this age [or world]" (2 Cor. 4:4), and in Ephesians 2:2 he describes Satan's power over the Ephesian believers before they were saved: "you followed the ways of this world and of the ruler of the kingdom of the air, the spirit who is now at work in those who are disobedient." Moreover, in a powerful and striking metaphor, which in the Greek suggests the image of a mother cradling her helpless child in her arms, John says that the whole world "is under the control of the evil one" (1 John 5:19). It is vital, however, correctly to understand the nature of Satan's rule over human beings, and to do so from two very important perspectives.

First, whatever power Satan may have over humanity is based on human sin. Men and women were not created to be subject to Satan but, because of their own rebellion against God, they have fallen under his tyranny, even if unconsciously for the most part. This is clearly implied in Colossians 2:13-15 (which we discuss more fully later), where Jesus' death for sins and the forgiveness of his people that flows from his death, result in his victory over the "powers and authorities" – among whom Satan is certainly to be numbered. The clear implication is this: that once sin is dealt with, the *powers and authorities* lose the power that enabled them to dominate human beings. They are *disarmed*. It is human sin that gives them their tyrannical power over men and women. Therefore, those who experience deliverance from sin inevitably also experience deliverance from Satan at the very same time.

Similarly, in John 14:30, as he faces his own imminent and violent death, Jesus says, "the prince of this world is coming" and then immediately adds, "he has no hold on me" – or, more literally, "he has nothing *in* me." The suggestion is that Satan does have something *in* other human beings that gives him power over them, but as he comes to attack Jesus, he has no power over him. Consequently, Jesus' death takes place, not because of any power Satan has over him, but because Jesus willingly carries out the will of his Father (14:31). The implication once again seems to be that Satan and the kingdom of darkness are parasites, feeding on human sin: Jesus has no sin and Satan therefore has no power over him. As soon as the guilt of their sin is dealt with through Christ, he has no control over the people of God either. When Satan wields power over human beings, he acts as a usurper; contrary to what is sometimes suggested, he has no 'legal rights' over them. Accordingly, when Jesus frees men and women through his death and resurrection, he does not buy Satan off – there is no ransom paid to him – but rather he drives him out (John 12:31). He deals with him as usurpers should always be dealt with.

Second, Satan only exercises any power – even over fallen humanity – to the extent that God allows him to do so. The world does not *belong* to Satan: it is God's world. God made it and he is sovereign over all that happens in it. However, men and women have rebelled and in consequence have fallen under the power of Satan – and God allows them to taste the bitter consequences of their sin. Nevertheless, God places limits on what Satan can do which Satan cannot exceed, and continues to direct human history in such a way as to secure Satan's defeat and the redemption of men and women.

The purpose and strategy of Satan

Satan is the supreme enemy of God and all his works. In all he does, his aim is to frustrate God's purposes and destroy everything he has made. His particular goal has been to alienate human beings from their creator by inciting them to rebel against him. The result is that they have lost their relationship with God – the one for whom they were made, and who is the only source of all that is good. Satan wants to bring about their eternal separation from God – everlasting death. This is expressed most clearly and concisely in Jesus' summary of his nature: "He was a murderer from the beginning, not holding to the truth, for there is no truth in him. When he lies, he speaks his native language, for he is a liar and the father of lies" (John 8:44). It was in the Garden of Eden that Satan, in the form of the serpent, revealed himself as both liar and murderer. Thus, he tempted the woman by lying – assuring her that she would not die if she ate the forbidden fruit, but would be like God. The purpose of the lie, and Satan's goal, was to bring about the death of the human couple despite his promise to them that it would not take place. The creation which God had pronounced very good was at once corrupted through the lies of Satan, whose purpose was to destroy it.

However, if Satan's original purpose was to destroy God's first creation, it is clear – and especially so in the New Testament – that he aims even more to devastate the new one too. In numerous ways, he attacks the people of God, his goal being not so much their physical destruction as the undermining of their faith and so of the restored relationship they have with God. So, Peter warns the readers of his letter to beware of their enemy, the devil, who seeks to devour them (1 Pet. 5:8), and James urges his readers to resist the devil (James 4:7). The book of Revelation demonstrates this particularly clearly when the dragon (Satan) attacks the woman and her offspring (the people of God), and raises up the two beasts, from the sea and from the earth, to bring about their destruction – which he seems indeed to achieve (Rev. 12-13). However, the book makes it clear that, although Satan may destroy the bodies of those who bear witness to Christ, they overcome Satan by remaining faithful even though they undergo physical death (Rev. 12:10). Indeed, because of the victory that Christ has already won, they overcome him by not loving their lives "so much as to shrink from death" (Rev. 12:11).

It is in the light of Satan's identity as murderer that his two main activities should be understood – tempting and accusing. He tempts to sin, and the penalty for sin is death; and he accuses people of sin in order to demand the execution of its penalty. In the Old Testament the purpose of his accusations and temptations – of David (1 Chron. 21:1), Job (Job 1-2), and Joshua the high priest (Zech. 3:1) – was to bring about the condemnation and judgement of those accused or tempted. In the New Testament his role as tempter and accuser becomes ever clearer, so that he is even given the title of tempter (Matt. 4:3; 1 Thess. 3:5). His temptations have a double thrust. On the one hand, they aim to keep the unredeemed mass of humanity enslaved in their sin. On the other, he wants to reclaim those who have been redeemed from sin by drawing them back into the very rebellion from which Christ has rescued them.

Meanwhile, at the heart of temptation there is always the lie, reflecting Satan's consistent character as liar (John 8:44). The temptation of Eve was based on a series of lies, the first of which was that her rebellion would not lead to death but to a status like that of God himself: "you will not surely die" (Gen. 3:5). Behind the first lie was therefore a second more treacherous one, namely that God's word is false and that he is not to be trusted. Beyond that was yet another more insidious lie: that God is not truly good and that his commands deprive human beings of their true happiness. They must, therefore, renounce his rule and assert their independence from him if they are to find fulfilment. This is the constant, universal character of temptation. However, true life is found in God alone, and such wilful rebellion necessarily brings about death.

These themes recur throughout the Bible, whenever Satan's activity as tempter comes into view. The lie is especially apparent in his inspiration of error. At one point Paul refers to those who "follow deceiving spirits and things taught by demons" (1 Tim. 4:1), indicating that Satan was the source of the false teaching which he had to combat in his own time. Similarly both the "false prophet" and the "man of iniquity" (Rev. 13; 2 Thess. 2:3-12) are inspired by Satan as they broadcast lies and alienate men and women from the truth which is found in Christ. Satan's goal is always to corrupt human minds with error, and so to draw them away from the true God. He inspires all false ideology and religion, including materialism and secularism, to accomplish these ends.

Moral sin is also rooted in lies: the notion that human happiness and fulfilment can be found in illicit sexual relationships, the possession of goods or power, or the pursuit of godless pleasure is false. This is not just about individual men and women, but whole societies are subject to Satan's deceit and manipulation, and he penetrates to the very heart of human worldviews. This is what lies at the root of Paul's denunciation of the Cretan culture of his day: "Cretans are always liars, evil brutes, lazy gluttons" (Titus 1:12). He sums it all up in his second letter to the Corinthians: by his lies Satan blinds "the minds of unbelievers, so that they cannot see the light of the gospel of the glory of Christ, who is the image of God" (2 Cor. 4:4).

Satan is also the accuser. The word 'devil' (*diabolos*), often used in Scripture, refers to this role. In the Old Testament he accuses Job by casting doubt on the sincerity of his worship (Job 1-2). He also accuses the high priest Joshua in Zechariah 3:1. In the New Testament he is described as "the accuser of our brothers, who accuses them before our God day and night" (Rev. 12:10). It is significant that in all of these references he accuses people before God, and not just in their own inner lives and consciences. Having tempted men and women to sin, he then accuses them before their creator of the sins they have committed, inevitably with a view to bringing about their condemnation and death. His roles as tempter, accuser and murderer are therefore intimately linked together – each one leading to the other. In this sense, the writer of the epistle to the Hebrews refers to Satan as the one "who holds the power of death" (2:14): he exploits human sin through temptation and accusation in order to bring about the death of men and women.

All of this gives the invisible world of the Bible a significance unknown in the traditional African worldview. The great threat that it presents to men and women is not so much physical (although that element is not absent) but spiritual. Satan and the powers of darkness want to bring about the eternal damnation of men and women by blinding them to the reality of their sinful condition, and keeping them in it. The menace is far graver than anything imagined in the traditional African worldview.

Satan, sin and suffering

As we have seen, African tradition attempts to explain suffering by invoking personal agency: 'There is always somebody'. The approach is based on the belief that reality ought to make sense, that there is order and meaning in the world, and that they can be discovered with the appropriate tools, such as divination. The perception that events *should* make sense seems to be profoundly rooted in human beings: we feel intuitively that there ought to be a reason for what happens, and find it difficult to live as if the universe was ultimately meaningless.

This is also evident in the Bible. When the disciples encountered the 'man born blind' they sought an explanation for his suffering by asking Jesus, "Rabbi, who sinned, this man or his parents, that he was born blind?" (John 9:2). Jesus did not criticise their attempt to make sense of the man's suffering, but he enlarged the range of possibilities which they should consider: "'Neither this man nor his parents sinned,' said Jesus, 'but this happened so that the work of God might be displayed in his life'" (John 9:3). Accordingly, the pursuit of meaning, the desire to understand that is evident in African thought, is not illegitimate. The issue is rather whether African tradition has been looking in the right direction to find that meaning.

For African peoples, spirits play a major role in the incidence of human pain and suffering, as do witches and sorcerers. They cause illness, accident, failure, drought and barrenness. There is some indication in the Bible too of their activity in this area, but it plays a much smaller part than it does in traditional Africa. In the Old Testament it is certainly Satan who caused the sufferings of Job – physical, material and emotional – although only with God's permission and within the tight limits that God established. In doing so, Satan is allowed to use both the weather and political events to destroy Job's family and wealth, as well as afflicting Job with a hideous illness (Job 1:13-19; 2:7). In the New Testament "a messenger of Satan" afflicted Paul with a "thorn in the flesh" (2 Cor. 12:7). Both expressions are somewhat mysterious, but the former would almost certainly have been understood to refer to a demon, and the latter probably means a physical illness of some sort. As in the case of Job, a man of God was physically afflicted by a demon. However, the language indicates that once again the whole incident took place in accordance with God's will and to further his purposes. Moreover, the way Paul expresses himself, using a verb in the passive voice – "there was given me a thorn in my flesh . . ." – means that God's will lay behind the affliction. Paul goes on to explain how it fulfilled God's good purpose in his own life and ministry, "For when I am weak, then I am strong" (2 Cor. 12:10).

Elsewhere in the New Testament, Jesus healed a woman "who had been crippled by a spirit for eighteen years" (Luke 13:10-17). The language is a little ambiguous and some take it to mean that she was possessed. However, the way in which Jesus responded to her suffering suggests that this was not the case. He touched her, which he is never recorded as doing in the case of those obviously possessed, he spoke to her directly rather than to an invasive demon, and he did not use the words he habitually used to expel a demon. It seems that the woman was bent double with curvature of the spine through being afflicted by a demon, rather than being actually *possessed*. Jesus goes on to describe her as "a daughter of Abraham, whom Satan has kept bound for eighteen long years", confirming the role of Satan in the suffering inflicted through demonic agency.

However, the problem in all of this is to identify the extent to which Satan may be responsible for *all* illnesses, as opposed to some isolated instances: how far can one generalize from relatively few cases? Some have argued that demons are indeed responsible for all cases of human suffering. In this connection, a particularly intriguing text is Peter's reference to Jesus' earthly ministry during his sermon to Cornelius and his household – "healing all who were under the power of the devil" (Acts 10:38). This may indeed suggest that Satan is responsible for every particular case of illness, but not necessarily so. It may instead be a reference to Jesus' deliverance of those actually possessed by demons, who were quite literally "under the power of the devil." Alternatively, Peter's words may reflect the fact that ultimately, human beings suffer illness because of sin, and Satan is the one who retains humanity captive in sin with all the consequences that implies. Certainly, the Bible does not unequivocally attribute all human suffering to direct demonic intervention. Indeed, the thrust of its teaching about the source of suffering points much more to the role of human sin rather than to demonic activity.

Accordingly, suffering is "the effluent of the fall, the result of a fallen world."[2] Human beings suffer because humanity as a whole bears the consequences of its own rebellion. It is here that the Bible puts its emphasis. This is all the more striking because some of the peoples who surrounded Israel actually did attribute suffering to hostile spirits. The Scriptures, however, – despite the few references to satanic or demonic involvement in illness already noted – did not follow them in that belief. Death, in particular, is explicitly identified as the consequence of sin (Gen. 2:16-17; John 8:21,24; Rom. 6:23) and so, by extension, all the associated evils – illness, accident, starvation and so on – should similarly be understood as deriving from sin. The Old Testament persistently returns to the retributive theory of suffering – in the law, the prophets and the historical writings.

However, the Bible also recognizes the ambiguities of human suffering. While in a general sense the existence of suffering within the world may be due to human rebellion, this does not necessarily mean that those who suffer most are the greatest rebels. Accordingly, while some psalms trace personal experience of suffering to specific sin and guilt, others recognize that visible punishment for sin is often neither swift

---

[2]D. A. Carson, *How Long O Lord: Reflections on Suffering and Evil* (Leicester: Inter-Varsity Press, 1990), 48.

nor obvious (Pss. 37; 73). The book of Job confronts the issue, and may be seen as a polemic against the view that behind every case of suffering there must have been some particular sin that produced it. The prophecy of Habakkuk wrestles with the same issue: "Why are you silent while the wicked swallow up those more righteous than themselves?" (Hab. 1:13). Similarly, in the New Testament there are indications that particular suffering may be associated with particular sin (John 5:14; 1 Cor. 11:30; Rev. 2:21-23), but certainly not in all cases, and sometimes the existence of such a connection is explicitly denied by Jesus himself (Luke 13:1-5; John 9:1-3).

In biblical theology, human suffering in all its forms exists because of the fall and its multiple consequences. Furthermore, sometimes human beings experience affliction as a direct result of their own individual sins, but one cannot simply conclude that an event of suffering is due to a specific sin. The 'innocent' may suffer while those more guilty than they often seem to escape retribution.

For the writers of Scripture, God is ultimately sovereign even in the incidence of suffering. If Job or Paul suffers through demonic attack, God has allowed that to happen and he sets the limits and duration of their trial. If Satan's "beast from the sea" attacks the people of God, even to the point of exterminating them, that power has been given to him for a period by God, as indicated by the repeated use of the passive voice (the so-called 'divine passive') in the early verses of Revelation 13. And if sin produces suffering, this does not occur because of an impassive, objective law or principle by which the universe operates, like the Hindu notion of *karma*.

Rather, it is the result of the judicial decree of the personal, sovereign creator.

It is, therefore, vitally important to notice that when godly people suffer in the Bible, they seek solutions to their pain in the presence of God. Job, for example, did not know the source of his suffering, which is revealed only to the reader of the book, but his sole response was to seek redress from God. Although many of the surrounding cultures would have had little hesitation in assuming demonic involvement, and the afflicted would therefore have sought to deal directly with the spirits concerned, there is no indication anywhere that Job thought in this way. Similarly, the apostle Paul was aware of the demonic nature of his "thorn in the flesh", but his response was to pray to God for relief and to wait for an answer from him. We return to this theme later.

Witchcraft and sorcery

The same is true of the Bible's approach to witchcraft and sorcery. The use of magic was widespread among Israel's neighbours:

> There can be no doubt that both the Old Testament and the New Testament were born in environments permeated with magical beliefs and practices.[3]

Indeed, much of the terminology used for magic practices in the Old Testament are Assyrian, Babylonian or Egyptian in origin. However, there is very little concrete description of magic practices in the Bible. If the Bible is fairly reticent about

---

[3] E. M. Yamauchi, 'Magic in the Biblical World' in *Tyndale Bulletin 34* (1983), 169.

the involvement of spirits in human suffering, it has even less to say about sorcerers. In fact, given the prevalence of contemporary beliefs about magic, the relative neglect of the issue in Scripture itself is highly significant. What it suggests is that the sovereign power of Yahweh inevitably tended to put the feeble performances of the practitioners of magic entirely in the shade.

Nevertheless, the potential efficacy of magic is assumed. The magicians of Egypt, for example, were able to imitate the first two plagues that Moses called down upon Egypt, although they were soon increasingly out of their depth (Ex. 8:18-19; 9:11). The eschatological "man of lawlessness" of whom Paul spoke, and whose arrival was anticipated shortly before Christ's return, would be able to perform signs (2 Thess. 2:9), as would the apocalyptic "beast from the earth" (Rev. 13:14). Significantly, both of these texts emphasize the satanic source of the power behind the signs in question. When Paul identified the magician Elymas as a "child of the devil" (Acts 13:10), he was similarly implying that it was the devil who empowered his sorcery.

However, what the Bible especially demonstrates, particularly through the stories of Joseph and Daniel, is the massive superiority of divine power over every expression of human magic. In both cases the power of the God of Israel is shown to be far superior to that of the magicians of Egypt and of Babylon respectively. Through his servants he is able to reveal what pagan divination cannot.

There are few biblical references to the aggressive use of magic, to the point that some have questioned whether it is there at all. However, there is a recognition that some people

attempted to harm others through occult means. Especially
significant is the story of Balaam (Num. 22-25), who was
apparently a pagan diviner and sorcerer. Balak's summons to
him, and his subsequent anger at Balaam's failure to curse
Israel, suggest that Balaam was reputedly able to manipulate
supernatural powers to harm his enemies and those of his
paymasters, by using the standard procedures of sorcery
(Num. 24:1). Accordingly, he was hired by Balak to curse the
Israelites, just as a sorcerer might be paid to bring misfortune
on an enemy:

> . . . come and put a curse on these people, because they
> are too powerful for me. Perhaps then I will be able to
> defeat them and drive them out of the country. For I
> know that those you bless are blessed, and those you
> curse are cursed (Num. 22:6).

However, what is striking in the story is that God intervened
in such a way that Balaam was compelled to bless rather
than curse his people. The projected occult aggression was
smothered as God reversed the evil intention of the two men.
Sorcery may therefore exist, but it too is subject to God's
sovereign will. "The only force that shapes the destiny of Israel
is God's plan, and no magical practices can thwart that divine
intention."[4]

Apart from Balaam there are few Old Testament references
to the aggressive use of magic. The "clever enchanter" of
Isaiah 3:3 was a magician of some sort, probably believed to
be able to inflict harm. Some of the ornaments described later

---

[4]H. C. Kee, *Medicine, Miracle and Magic in New Testament Times* (Cambridge:
Cambridge University Press, 1986), 18.

in the chapter (3:18-21) may have been fetishes intended to protect the wearer against sorcery.

The condemnation of magic activity by Ezekiel is significant but enigmatic (Ezek. 13:17-23):

> Woe to the women who sew magic charms on all their wrists and make veils of various lengths for their heads in order to ensnare people . . . I am against your magic charms with which you ensnare people like birds and I will tear them from your arms; I will set free the people that you ensnare like birds (18,20).

The prophet certainly had in mind female diviners who were communicating lies, but there seems to have been more to it than that. They were not only lying to their hearers, but also using magic spells to control, and perhaps kill, them – "more like witches and sorceresses who practised strange magic arts."[5] The bands of cloth and veils were apparently part of the ritual that they followed, magic amulets "intended to bring about untimely deaths."[6] "The practice of the false prophetesses was to tie bands of cloth to their wrists and place veils over their heads as they cast spells over people's lives in order to bind them and hunt them down." [7] As the prophecy is addressed to the exiles, the practice of sorcery among them may well testify to the influence of Babylonian culture.

References to aggressive magic are equally few in the New Testament. Ephesus was well known as a centre of

---

[5] J. B. Taylor, *Ezekiel* (Leicester: Inter-Varsity Press, 1969), 123.

[6] D. E. Aune, 'Magic', in G.W. Bromiley (ed.), *ISBE*, vol. III (Grand Rapids: Eerdmans, 1986), 215.

[7] R. H. Alexander, 'Ezekiel' in F. E. Gaebelein (ed.), *The Expositor's Bible Commentary vol 6* (Grand Rapids: Zondervan, 1986).

magic, however, and it was probably for this reason that Paul emphasized Christ's superiority over every conceivable source of power in the occult world (Eph. 1:20-21). It is interesting that in doing so Paul neither affirms nor denies the power of sorcery, and certainly does not minimise or deride the fears of the Ephesian believers. Nor, however, does he affirm all the details of their witchcraft beliefs, whatever they may have been – and they were certainly very varied and complex. His concern is rather to demonstrate that, whatever hostile occult power there might be, Christ is infinitely greater and is able to guard his people, who are already seated "with him in the heavenly realms" (2:6). His purpose is so to plant truth in their minds – the truth of Christ's triumph and sovereign reign – that their fears would be allayed. Ephesus was also one of the churches to which the book of Revelation was addressed, and sorcery is mentioned there a number of times.

In Galatians, *pharmakeia*, translated 'witchcraft' in the New International Version of the Bible, is among "the acts of the sinful nature" (Gal. 5:19-21). The word *pharmakon* which is very close to it, initially meant a drug, sometimes used in erotic magic, but associated terms "refer more often to magical material used for purposes of hate rather than love."[8] Hence there is little doubt that *pharmakeia* is correctly translated as witchcraft. Accordingly in the culture which the Galatians shared, one of the forms that sin took was witchcraft or sorcery – the attempt to use occult means to harm another person.

---

[8]Yamauchi, 'Magic in the Biblical World', 181.

Thus, Paul recognised the reality of the act and its hostile intent, but he does not discuss its exact nature nor comment on its efficacy.

To summarize, the Bible acknowledges that there are those who seek to harm their fellow human beings by means of witchcraft and sorcery. If that were not so, it would not condemn such activities, which it does in both testaments. Moreover, the Bible also confirms that practitioners of magic are indeed able to produce certain phenomena through Satan's power. Insofar as witchcraft is a form of magic, it is plausible to suppose that in some situations it too may be used effectively to harm others. Nevertheless, there are only a very few biblical references that imply its effectiveness, including Ezekiel 13 and the story of Balaam. Thus, while the Bible does not deny its possible effectiveness, it does not give it a great deal of attention.

Furthermore, if the Bible gives only very scant support to the possibility of witchcraft, it offers none to the many and varied culture-specific notions of witchcraft activity found in traditional religious belief, whether in Africa or elsewhere in the world. Accepting the notion that some people may cause harm to others by occult means, does not mean accepting, for example, that witches eat the souls of human beings, or consume those who are buried and in the grave. The Bible does not encourage a credulous disposition, but an attitude that critically examines claims from a biblical perspective.

Moreover, nowhere does the Bible suggest that witches and sorcerers are *major* causes of human suffering. A biblical worldview will not see witchcraft as a generalised cause of suffering, as is true of much African tradition. Suffering is due to sin: it is sin – not the witch – that is the great enemy of humanity because it has separated men and women from their Creator as a result of the fall, which has also had an impact on the whole of created reality. Witchcraft belief moves responsibility for our trials away from ourselves and onto third parties. We become victims of witches, rather than the guilty men and women that we truly are.

In this connection it is instructive to consider certain psalms. Some interpreters have been inclined to see the 'evildoers' found in some psalms as sorcerers who have caused the illness of the psalmist, and from whom he seeks deliverance and protection. Two psalms are especially relevant in this connection, 38 and 41. However, there are telling arguments against such an interpretation of them.

First, in both psalms the enemies emerge as a result of the illness of the psalmist. They want to gloat over the sufferer and to profit from his illness, but in *neither* case are they identified as causes of that illness. Second, in both cases the psalmist explicitly, even emphatically, identifies his own sin and guilt as the cause of his illness. This is indeed what we would expect from a godly man writing within the context of a biblical worldview:

> *Because of your wrath* there is no health in my body; my bones have no soundness *because of my sin. My guilt* has overwhelmed me like a burden too heavy to bear. My wounds fester and are loathsome *because of my sinful folly* (Ps. 38:3-5);

"LORD, have mercy on me; heal me, *for I have sinned* against you" (Ps. 41:4).

However, the use of sorcery of any kind is certainly denounced in the Bible, and those who do such things are among the condemned who will never enter the new Jerusalem (Rev. 21:8; 22:15). The practice of sorcery and witchcraft is sin which, like all other sin, leads to death, and so must be confessed and repented of. However, the whole issue receives very little attention because God's people were so aware of the almighty reign of God and Christ over all creation.

This brings us back to the critical issue that shapes any response to suffering, that of worldview. In the traditional African understanding of reality God has a relatively small active role in the world and, as a result, human beings feel themselves threatened by all sorts of hidden enemies, including spirits and sorcerers. They must, therefore, defend themselves, or seek to appease or destroy their attackers. The biblical worldview, while recognising the existence of spirits and sorcerers, as well as the harm that they might do to human beings, understands them in the context of a cosmos ruled by a sovereign God who is intimately involved in his creation, and who is good and constantly accessible to his own people. The difference of worldview necessarily produces a huge difference in the nature of the response to suffering. The way people understand the world around them and its workings determines the way they live and act.

Demonic possession

A particular and devastating expression of Satan's enslavement of humanity is 'possession' by demons or unclean spirits. Most human beings are not 'possessed': they are sinners and, unless redeemed through the work of Christ, they remain under Satan's power. However, possession is apparently an extreme manifestation of Satan's tyranny, and an exceptional and unusual phenomenon – although perhaps less unusual in some parts of the world than others. It is nevertheless one to which the synoptic gospels and Acts refer, and which has been found in cultures and societies right across the world, including Africa.

In the Bible, cases of possession are found in the synoptic gospels and Acts; the only possible Old Testament case is that of King Saul (see also 1 Sam. 16:14-23; 18:6-11; 19:8-10), although his symptoms do not coincide exactly with those recorded in the New Testament. The term itself, 'possession', is not used in the New Testament, which speaks rather of 'having a demon', or 'being in an impure spirit', or 'being troubled by a demon', or 'being demonised'. Nevertheless, 'possession' is an appropriate term to use in view of what apparently happens to a person who 'has a demon'. Moreover, the New Testament gives no theoretical definition of the condition but rather focuses on the symptoms experienced by possessed people. In general, it seems that when a spirit 'possesses' a person it takes total control of them, replacing their will by its own so that it can direct them. It is somewhat like hypnotism, and the similarity suggests that there is a mechanism within human beings which may allow a foreign will – whether human or spirit – to seize control of them.

The New Testament suggests that possession was well known and easily identified at the time of Jesus. In Mark's gospel, for example, when a woman came to Jesus to ask him to help her daughter who was possessed by a demon,

Jesus unquestioningly accepted her diagnosis without even seeing the girl concerned (Mark 7:24-30). However, the gospel accounts of possessed people allow us to identify some key symptoms. Thus, there is the presence of a *personality alien to the victim,* which is often indicated when the demon – rather than the possessed individual – speaks. That was so with the Gerasene demoniac (Mark 5:1-20; Matt. 8:28-34; Luke 8:26-39), and the demoniac of Capernaum (Mark 1:21-8; compare with Mark 3:11). In Mark 9:14-29 the demon does not speak, but displays its presence by the self-destructive behaviour of its victim (9:18, 20, 22; compare with Matt. 17:14-21; Luke 9:37-43). Secondly, the possessed person often displays *a tendency to self-harm* under the influence of the spirit. The Gerasene demoniac cut himself with stones (Mark 5:5), and the demon which possessed the epileptic boy threw him into fire and water (Mark 9:22), convulsed and destroyed him (Luke 9:39). Thirdly, possession was also often linked with serious *physical symptoms,* including epilepsy (Mark 9:14-29; Matt. 17:14-21; Luke 9:37-43), dumbness (Matt. 9:32-34), even blindness *and* dumbness (Matt. 12:22), while the daughter of the Canaanite woman "was suffering terribly from demon-possession" (Matt. 15:22). The presence of a demon thus produced the progressive disintegration of the individual at the physical level, as well as the mental and emotional – another reminder that Satan's purpose is destruction and death. Fourthly, the demoniacs in the gospels often possessed some *extraordinary ability.* The Gerasene demoniac had exceptional strength: he "tore the chains apart and broke the irons on his feet. No-one was strong enough to subdue him" (Mark 5:4). In other cases, there was a remarkable knowledge, as the demons recognized the true identity of Jesus when even the disciples had not grasped it. Without being instructed, the demoniac in the synagogue of Capernaum called him "the Holy One of God" (Mark 1:24), and the Gerasene demoniac "Son of the Most High God" (Mark 5:7; Luke 8:28; Matt. 8:29). In Acts the slave girl who had a spirit could predict the future, and knew who Paul and Silas were – "servants of the Most High God" (Acts 16:16-17). Jesus made the demons be silent because "whenever the evil spirits saw him, they fell down before him and cried out, 'You are the Son of God'" (Mark 3:11). Finally, possession also produced *bizarre conduct*. However, it is necessary to distinguish between possession and simple madness. Signs of mental derangement accompanied possession, but that does not mean that people believed that all such derangement was caused by possession. In an early summary of Jesus' ministry, Matthew refers to the way in which he healed both lunatics and demoniacs (Matt. 4:24); so all madness was not regarded as possession, but possession does seem invariably to have produced some symptoms of madness. The Gerasene demoniac did not wear clothes and lived among the tombs, separated from human society (Luke 8:27), and he cried out and cut himself (Mark 5:5). The demoniac in the Capernaum synagogue cried out during the service (Mark 1:23-4).

The gospels suggest three other significant features of possession. First, it was not necessarily continuous. In Mark 9:18 (Luke 9:39) the demon's attacks were apparently sporadic: "whenever it seizes him it throws him to the ground." By contrast, the Gerasene suffered continually: "night and day among the tombs and in the hills he would cry out and cut himself with stones" (Mark 5:5). Second, there are *degrees of possession*. The Canaanite woman said her daughter was suffering *terribly* from possession (Matt. 15:22). The parable of the return of the unclean spirit (Matt. 12:43-5) and the example of the Gerasene demoniac also show that people could be possessed by many spirits, with correspondingly more serious consequences for those so afflicted. Third, no explicit connection is made between possession and sin. So, on the one hand, sin is not attributed to possession. The biblical response to sin is always repentance, and never the expulsion of demons. On the other hand, possession is not explicitly attributed to sin in the Bible. It may be that engagement in some occult practices which are themselves sinful, does open an individual to spirit possession – that such engagement is in fact an invitation to spirit invasion. However, in the case of the young Canaanite girl it seems unlikely that sinful conduct was the cause of her possessed state.

Biblical and African descriptions of possession are strikingly similar. In both cases an invisible agent has taken control of a human being; there is strange behaviour often including a flight from human society and self-inflicted harm; there may be physical illness; and there may also be remarkable insights or feats of strength. However, differing perspectives on the nature of spirits means that the biblical and the traditional African responses are almost totally different. In the African context, while initial spirit possession may be seen as an illness which has to be dealt with, it is very often the beginning of a permanent relationship with the spirit which can lead to a role of importance within society – such as diviner or shaman – or at least to participation in a spirit cult. Moreover, possession may very often be positively valued for its own sake. Thus, it is not simply an evil to be eliminated, if it is ever that at all; through negotiation with the spirit it may be turned to the advantage of the possessed person and those around them. The same approach – sometimes termed 'voluntary possession' – is clearly evident in some pagan cultures of the first century, and in many others. For example, the case of spirit possession that Paul encountered in Philippi enabled the victim, a slave girl, to fulfil the role of medium, which was a source of profit to her owners (Acts 16:16). However, from a New Testament perspective possession is simply an evil, an extreme expression of satanic domination of an individual. The only appropriate response is one of deliverance – the expulsion of the spirit and the liberation of its victim. The critical issue once again is that of worldview: the actual phenomenon of possession seems to have been the same in Africa as it was in first century Israel, but differing conceptions of the nature of the spirit world lead to radically different responses.

Communicating with the dead

In traditional African thought, communication with the spirit world, particularly with the ancestors, has tended to be an accepted part of life. The dead continue to be a part of the community of the living, and they communicate with their descendants through dreams and suffering, while the living respond with sacrifice and invocation – and sometimes even reproach if they feel they are being treated unfairly. All such communication is prohibited in the Bible, and is understood as depriving God of the place he should hold in the lives of human beings. Two texts are particularly important in this regard. First, in Deuteronomy Moses forbids all contact with diviners and mediums, or anyone who seeks contact with the dead.

> Let no-one be found among you who . . . practises divination or sorcery, interprets omens, engages in witchcraft, or casts spells, or who is a medium or spiritist or who consults the dead (Deut. 18:10-11).

Instead of engaging in such practices, "The LORD your God will raise up for you a prophet like me from among your own brothers" (Deut. 18:15). In short, God's people are not to seek wisdom and guidance from the dead, but from God himself. With much the same reasoning, Isaiah addresses a question to his hearers:

> When men tell you to consult mediums and spiritists, who whisper and mutter, should not a people enquire of their God? Why consult the dead on behalf of the living? (Isa. 8:19).

Once again, it is consciousness of the presence of the living God among them that should make all the difference between Israel and her neighbours. The people of God have no cause to consult dead people because God himself speaks to them through his appointed spokesmen. The crucial issue is worldview: Israel's understanding of the nature of reality, specifically the nature of the living God, means that pursuit of contact with the dead is ridiculous as well as being rebellious.

Does the Bible nevertheless suggest that the dead may contact the living, as many African peoples have believed? The evidence is slender. The only passage which suggests the possibility is the story of King Saul's encounter with the 'witch' – who should more accurately be referred to as a medium or necromancer – of Endor (1 Sam. 28:7-25). The story is clear that the dead Samuel did indeed appear to Saul, but there is much in the narrative to suggest that the event was quite exceptional, even in the experience of the medium herself. When Samuel actually appears in the course of the séance she is clearly astounded: "When the woman saw Samuel, she cried out at the top of her voice" (1 Sam. 28:12). It was an event the like of which she had never experienced before, for a dead person really had appeared! She then lost control of her own séance as Samuel entered directly into communication with Saul without her mediation. Therefore, if the story teaches anything about communication with the dead, it is that mediums do not normally establish contact with them – perhaps never establish such contact except in this extraordinary case. This might imply that, insofar as such people do have communication with some sort of spirit beings, it is probably with demons who belong to Satan's kingdom rather than with the dead. It would also be consistent with biblical teaching about the state of the dead between death and resurrection, where believers go directly into the presence of Christ while unbelievers go to a place of judgement. In neither case do they continue in a state of proximity to living human beings.

Conclusion

The African worldview rightly recognizes the existence of the spiritual realm, and its frequently negative impact on the lives of men and women; the invisible world constitutes a threat to the lives and wellbeing of the living. Thus, spirits and sorcerers attack, and the living adopt a variety of defences and strategies to protect themselves. The Bible also testifies to the existence of spirits and the threat that some of them pose to human beings. However, the biblical picture is radically different from that of traditional Africa.

First, the biblical writers understand the invisible world as a monarchy in which God rules over spirits and men, both good and evil. The traditional African worldview gives the impression of an anarchy of spirits and of invisible forces, over which God may in principle be supreme, but in which he rarely if ever intervenes. This means that, second, the spirit world in the Bible receives much less attention than it does in traditional Africa. This is because the horizon of the biblical writers is so filled with a sense of God's greatness and his sovereign reign over all his creation. All created spirits – as well as the activity of witches or sorcerers – inevitably become issues of much smaller concern. The apparent fixation of the traditional African worldview with spirits, witchcraft and sorcery, is in sharp contrast to this biblical reticence. Third, witchcraft and sorcery may be realities, but the Bible does not attribute to them the importance as an explanation of human suffering that African tradition does. There is no biblical justification for witch-hunts and the accusation of witches. People like Job and Paul took their sufferings to God for solution, rather than pursuing lesser spirits or sorcerers. Fourth, while African conceptions of the spirit world are often complex, and human beings depend on the skills of diviners to navigate that world, the Bible offers a much simpler picture with a clear-cut division within the invisible world between beings who have remained faithful to God and those who have rebelled. The real danger comes from the latter group under the leadership of the devil and his agents. Finally, in biblical terms, the danger posed by Satan is not so much the threat he presents to the physical wellbeing of human beings, but rather his desire to separate men and women eternally from the presence of God. Satan may indeed use physical affliction – although never outside of the sovereign control of God – but he has objectives far more grave than causing simple physical pain. At this point, the African worldview has only a superficial understanding of the profoundly evil intent of Satan and the agents he commands.

Questions for further reflection

1. What are the principal differences between a biblical conception of the spirit world and that of traditional Africa?

2. "The Lord reigns" (Ps. 96:10), but Satan is "the prince of this world" (John 12:31; 14:30; 16:11). How can we reconcile these two biblical declarations?

3. Should we fear the power of Satan?

4. To what extent is all temptation really rooted in lies?

5. Is Satan responsible for human sins?

6. What causes illness: Satan, demons, sin, germs and microbes, or God?

7. Is communication possible between living and dead human beings?

CHAPTER 4

THE VICTORY OF CHRIST

It was along another line that he was tested at this time, and that more and more seriously. In the ardour of his faith he had taken it for granted that God's time had come for the blessing he longed to see among the Lisu. . . But in reality the opposite was the case. The people at Little River were hospitable and friendly as before, but showed no added interest in spiritual things. Rain and mist in the mountains might be depressing; but as the days and weeks wore on, he realized that there were influences of another kind to be reckoned with.

For strange uncertainty began to shadow his inward life. All he had believed and rejoiced in became unreal, and even his prayers seemed to mock him as the answers faded into nothingness . . . In his solitude, depression such as he had never known before closed down upon him.

Deeply were the foundations shaken in those days and nights of conflict, until Fraser realized that behind it all were the 'powers of darkness', seeking to overwhelm him. He had dared to invade Satan's kingdom, undisputed for ages. At first, vengeance had fallen on the Lisu inquirers, an easy prey. Now, he himself was attacked—and it was war to the death, spiritually. No one knew

*about it or imagined what the lonely pioneer was facing; that in
his extremity he was even tempted, and that persistently, to make
an end of it all . . . it was then, when the rainy season was at
its dreariest, that a messenger came from Tengyueh with letters
and papers, one of which brought him light. Someone . . had sent
him a copy of The Overcomer, a magazine with which Fraser was
unfamiliar. Its appearance in the poor little shack in those Lisu
mountains was surely timed by Omnipotent Love! for it set forth
the very truth needed in that strange conflict, and 'the truth shall
make you free'.*

*The fact that came home to Fraser as he pored over the
welcome pages, reading and re-reading every word, was that Satan
is indeed a conquered foe. Christ, our risen Lord, has in very
truth 'bruised his head' upon the cross of shame. 'Having put off
from Himself (through his death) the principalities and powers, He
made a show of them openly, triumphing over them in it.' This he
had held before, as a matter of doctrine. Now, it shone out for him
in letters of light that victory is ours. Satan had desired to have him
—determined, as he realized, upon wrecking him as a missionary,
then and there. No words could tell what the long struggle in the
dark had been. But now the Mighty Victor took him by the hand.*

*Long years before . . Fraser had responded in obedience to the
claims of that Glorious One Who, for him, had died upon the Cross.
Now, in the Lisu mountains, he responded again and yet more
deeply to the liberating power of the same Cross. 'They overcame
him (the great enemy) by the blood of the Lamb and by the word*

of their testimony.' There, in that poor shack, the victory was won that was to mean life to thousands. [1]

In the Old Testament, God is sometimes portrayed as a warrior who comes to defeat his enemies and those of his people. When the Israelites celebrated their deliverance at the Red Sea, they worshipped their redeemer in words which reflect that conception: "The LORD is a warrior; the LORD is his name" (Ex. 15:3). In the New Testament, the divine warrior becomes incarnate in the person of Jesus Christ, and the spiritual forces of darkness are among the enemies he engages in combat. In his first epistle, John expresses this very clearly: "the reason the Son of God appeared was to destroy the devil's work" (1 John 3:8). He is therefore the great spiritual warrior who has won the definitive victory over Satan and all the powers of evil and is God's final answer to the real menace presented by the invisible world. For believers, this means that he is the end of all negotiation and compromise with that world – whether through diviners, fetishes, sacrifices or whatever. As Christians find themselves facing spiritual adversaries, they do not fight in the hope of eventual triumph but rather with the assurance that victory has already been won through Christ.

The New Testament points us to five principal moments in Christ's warfare against Satan, in each of which he is victorious and which together bring about Satan's total downfall.

---

[1] H. Taylor, *Behind the Ranges: Fraser of Lisuland* (London: China Inland Mission, 1963 [1944]), 88-91. Reproduced by permission of OMF International, Singapore.

Temptation

Immediately after his baptism and anointing for ministry
by the Holy Spirit, Jesus went into the desert where Satan
tempted him. Matthew makes it clear that the spiritual conflict
he faced there did not come about simply as a result of the
devil's initiative, but was rather the fulfilment of God's own
purpose for his Son: "Then Jesus was led by the Spirit into the
desert to be tempted by the devil" (Matt. 4:1). The Holy Spirit
led Jesus into the desert with the specific purpose that he
should be tempted: the temptations did not happen by chance
and they were not simply imposed on Jesus by Satan. Without
engaging in too detailed an analysis of the temptations, their
significance needs to be understood from two perspectives of
immense importance.

First, in facing Satan's temptations Jesus was representing
humanity as the *second Adam*. The notion of the second Adam
is one that Paul in particular uses to explain the work of
Jesus (Rom. 5:12-21; 1 Cor. 15:20-22): he is the one who
overcame sin where the first Adam failed. Through that
victory he became the head of a new, redeemed and justified
humanity, just as the first Adam was the head of the old,
fallen and condemned humanity. Therefore, in his temptations
– in which he acted as representative of that recreated human
race – Jesus had to overcome Satan at the very point at
which Adam had been defeated. What took place in his desert
confrontation with the devil was something of a re-run of
the earliest and most critical moments of human history. It
is particularly significant that Jesus' victory over the devil
was a moral one: it was not accomplished by superior force
but by offering to God that perfect obedience which Adam,

as first representative of the race, had failed to bring. The devil's power over men and women is based on human sin, and so Jesus had first to defeat Satan at that point – by resisting temptation and submitting to God's will on behalf of the men and women whom he had come to redeem. That initial victory was the essential basis on which his ultimate conquest of Satan would be completed.

Second, there is also in this incident a very clear parallel with Israel's desert experience. Jesus faces Satan not only as the second Adam but also as the new Israel. Israel was brought out of Egypt as the "son of God" (Ex. 4:22-23; Hosea 11:1), and then led through the desert where the nation was tempted for 40 years – and repeatedly fell. In a similar way, after himself being proclaimed as Son of God (Matt. 3:17; Mark 1:11; Luke 3:22), Jesus was also led into the desert by the Spirit and was tempted there for 40 days, but in his case without giving way. Significantly, he responded to each of the temptations with quotations from the book of Deuteronomy (8:3; 6:13; 6:16), which inevitably recall the desert wanderings of Israel. Symbolically, at the very outset of his ministry he repeated Israel's experience. He confronted Satan as the embodiment of a renewed Israel, representative of a new people of God who would at last offer to God that faithfulness which the old Israel constantly failed to give even from the very beginning of her nationhood.

Following on from this, two aspects of the *content* of Jesus' temptations are also particularly important. First, Satan seeks to test Jesus' consciousness of his identity. There is again a parallel here with the temptation in Eden. In the garden Satan began his assault on Eve by casting doubt on the word of God,

using a question to do so, "Did God really say . . .?" (Gen. 3:1).
In the desert he uses a similar tactic when he prefaces two
of the temptations with an allusion to the words with which
God had just declared Jesus' divine sonship at his baptism,
"You are my son whom I love" (Luke 3:22). Satan's use of the
conditional clause – "*if* you are the Son of God . . ." – has a
purpose similar to that of the question addressed to Eve in the
garden. He brings the divine declaration, and with it Jesus'
unique filial relationship, under the spotlight, and challenges
Jesus to test its meaning and possibilities – even its reality. It
was a vital issue because Jesus' whole ministry would be built
upon his profound consciousness of his identity as the Son of
God. He came consciously in the name of the Father (John
5:37); as the Son it was he alone who knew the Father and had
the power to make him known to others (Matt. 11:27; Luke
10:22). What he spoke was what he had seen in the Father's
presence (John 8:38). In the same way, his works were those
he had seen his Father doing, and he acted in total dependence
on him (John 5:19). It was this deep awareness of sonship
that undergirded his mission: the fulfilment of his work was
inseparably related to his self-understanding. By challenging
him at the very core of his divine identity, Satan was trying
to cripple that work at the most foundational level.

Second, an underlying tendency of Satan's temptations
was to cause Jesus to deviate from the path of the cross –
from the heart of the mission he had come to carry out. All of
them imply in one way or another that suffering may not be
necessary for the realisation of his work. Therefore, he does
not have to experience hunger but can use his divine powers to
satisfy his personal needs and avoid discomfort. Similarly, by

an extraordinary demonstration of power – throwing himself from the temple pinnacle – he can draw followers to himself instead of enduring the incomprehension and even hostility of his own people. Finally, by bowing to Satan – going the devil's way and using his means – he can painlessly establish his authority over the world. Later on, when Peter challenged Jesus' assertion that he must be rejected and killed, Jesus recognized instantly the voice of Satan behind his disciple. Once again, just as he had in the desert, Satan was luring Jesus away from the mission of suffering for which he had come. Jesus reacted accordingly: "Get behind me, Satan!" (Matt. 16:23; Mark 8:33).

There is nothing trivial or incidental about what took place in the desert: it was a pivotal moment in Jesus' ministry. Just as he had done in Eden, Satan's attack in the desert struck at the foundations of Jesus' identity and his mission, his person and his work, but Satan failed.

Expulsion

At the time of Jesus' ministry there were people in Israel possessed by spirits, perhaps especially in the region of Galilee where much of his work took place. A major part of that ministry was the liberation of such people, their deliverance from the power of the spirits who controlled and wanted to destroy them. It is clear that he was not the only person engaged in such work at the time (Matt. 12:27; Mark 9:38; Luke 9:49; 11:19), but the synoptic gospels suggest that what he did was quite exceptional, and particularly in two respects.

First, he drove out demons in large numbers. Outside the gospels there are very few references to exorcisms in the first- century world, and even less evidence of the *successful* expulsion of demons; nor do we know the names of contemporary exorcists, with perhaps one or two exceptions. However, it is clear that Jesus was both very active and also very successful in freeing people from demonic oppression. There are four distinct narratives of liberation from demon possession in the synoptic gospels – the largest single group of miracles recorded in the gospels – and there are also references to this aspect of his work in the summaries of his ministry which the gospel writers give from time to time (Matt. 4:23-25; 8:16-17; Mark 1:32-34, 39; 3:11; Luke 4:40-41). It is particularly significant that Jesus' enemies felt obliged to come up with some explanation for his very obvious success in liberating possessed people. They were clearly unable to deny the fact that the victims of demons were being freed, and so they were reduced to explaining his remarkable success by claiming that he was acting through the power of Beelzebub, or Satan (Matt. 12:24; Mark 3:22; Luke 11:15).

Second, he delivered the victims of possession with an apparent effortlessness, which contrasted sharply with the practices of contemporary exorcists. There are documents that survive from the period with directions for the expulsion of evil spirits. They show that exorcists would expect to use special incantations, often involving the repetition of meaningless magic words. There would be special rites that had to be followed to the letter. Exorcists would invoke the name of a power source, a powerful spirit, or even the name of a god, in order to coerce the demon into submission. And, finally, they would also try to force the demon to speak and disclose its name, as it was believed that knowledge and use of its name would give them power over it. Jesus did none of this. There is no evidence in the gospels that he even prayed when he drove out spirits and, rather than make them speak, he commanded them to remain silent (Luke 4:41). The only occasion on which he did ask the name of a demon, he did not use it in the subsequent expulsion (Mark 5:9). He simply told them to leave: "he drove out the spirits with a word" (Matt. 8:16). The extraordinary nature of his 'technique' was another factor that amazed those who witnessed his work: "He even gives orders to evil spirits and they obey him" (Mark 1:27). It is probably because of the effortless and absolute power with which he expelled demons that the gospel writers never use the verb to *exorcise* to describe what he did, although they do use it to refer to efforts by the demons to control *him*. When Jesus encounters the Gerasene demoniac, the demons' words suggest a useless attempt on their part to resist him through the standard language of exorcism. They used both the verb often translated to exorcise, and they also invoked a power source to defend themselves against him: "I adjure [exorcise] you, by God, do not torment me" (Mark 5:7). For the gospel writers, Jesus' ministry could not be put in the same category as that of contemporary 'exorcists' – it was totally different in nature and intent, which leads to the *meaning* of his expulsion of demons.

While the gospels do not use the verb *exorcise* to refer to Jesus' expulsions, they do use another which is often translated *rebuke*, and which no other contemporary writers used to refer to the expulsion of demons (Matt. 17:18; Mark 1:25; 3:12; 9:25; Luke 4:35; 9:42). The Greek verb is the equivalent of a Semitic term used by some Jewish authors to speak of the way in which God himself *rebukes*, and indeed defeats, forces that oppose him. Moreover, in Mark 1:25 the Greek sentence structure puts an emphasis on the word *rebuke*, in a way that may well have communicated its special significance to the readers. The use of this particular word therefore suggests that in driving out demons, Jesus was demonstrating the power of God, crushing his enemies, and saving those who were oppressed by them. There is "an overtone of divine authority" here.[2] Similarly, other than in the gospels, the Greek verb translated *drive out* is nowhere used of the expulsion of demons, but in the Septuagint (the Greek translation of the Old Testament) it is used to refer to God's action in driving out an enemy.

This leads on to Jesus' own explicit interpretation of what was taking place when demons were expelled from their victims. As we have noted, his enemies claimed that he drove out demons by the power of Beelzebub, the prince of demons (Matt. 12:22- 32; Mark 3:22-30; Luke 11:14-23). Jesus' reply pointed to the illogical nature of such an argument. In possessing people demons were acting precisely as agents of the prince of demons – they were carrying out his will and holding 'territory' in his name. Beelzebub was therefore hardly likely to co-operate in their expulsion: if he did so, he would be fighting against himself and diminishing his own realm. Accordingly, Jesus must be acting with the help of a quite different supernatural power – that of the Holy Spirit (Matt. 12:28), the very finger of God (Luke 11:20; compare with Ex. 8:19) – and that could only mean that the kingdom of God had come, a truth which was right at the heart of

---

[2]C. E. B. Cranfield, *Mark* (Cambridge: Cambridge University Press, 1959), 77.

the message he was preaching. The expulsion of demons was therefore tangible evidence of the truth of his message, and evidence too of his real identity. It meant that in Jesus Christ, God had come in power to vanquish his foes and free their victims. This both coincided with the evangelists' use of the verb *rebuke* as discussed above, and also fulfilled Old Testament anticipation of God's climactic intervention to deal not only with human foes but also spiritual ones:

> In that day the LORD will punish the powers in the heavens above and the kings on the earth below. They will be herded together like prisoners bound in a dungeon; they will be shut up in prison and be punished after many days. . . for the LORD Almighty will reign on Mount Zion and in Jerusalem (Isa. 24:21- 23).

Jesus' response to the disciples' joy at being able to drive out demons in the course of their mission has very much the same meaning:

> . . . the seventy-two returned with joy and said, 'Lord, even the demons submit to us in your name.' He replied, 'I saw Satan fall like lightning from heaven' (Luke 10:17-18).

In his reply Jesus is saying that the submission of the demons to the disciples was again evidence of Satan's own fall from power. His disciples' expulsion of evil spirits had the same essential meaning as his own: Satan was giving way before the onslaught of the kingdom of God, and being deprived of his possessions. Moreover, in the following verse – "I have given you authority to trample on snakes and scorpions and to overcome all the power of the enemy; nothing will harm you" – Jesus used symbolic language to give his disciples authority to continue to advance against Satan as their ministry brought redemption to those who were subject to him.

Death

The crucifixion of Jesus is the central point not just for the gospel narratives but also for the whole of the New Testament. It is primarily understood by the New Testament writers as a propitiatory sacrifice offered up to God to make atonement for human sin, explicitly affirmed in one of the very earliest and most succinct Christian confessions of faith – "Christ died for our sins according to the Scriptures" (1 Cor. 15:3-4). However, it also has powerful implications for Satan and the forces of darkness, being the climactic moment in Jesus' struggle with them. Especially important in this respect are the words of Jesus towards the end of his ministry, recorded in John 12:31-32:

> Now is the time for judgment on this world; now the prince of this world will be driven out. But I, when I am lifted up from the earth, will draw all men to myself.

Unlike the synoptic writers, John's gospel contains no narrative describing the deliverance of possessed people from demonic power, nor any general reference to that dimension of Jesus' ministry. However, in the words just quoted, Jesus uses the verb *drive out*, to describe the expulsion of Satan from the world, a verb that is characteristically employed in the synoptic gospels to refer to the driving out of demons. By implication, therefore, John identifies the cross as the definitive act of demonic expulsion by which Satan himself, the ruler of demons, is driven out of the world that he tyrannises as 'prince'. As a result of that, his victims, whom he enslaved by exploiting their own sin, are liberated, and Jesus draws them to himself.

However, it is clearly paradoxical that the death of Jesus should constitute his victory over Satan: death invariably signifies defeat rather than victory. Thus, the notion that Jesus' death constituted Satan's defeat needs some explanation. In addition to this brief reference in John's gospel, several other biblical passages also display the cross as victory over Satan, and suggest how it came about.

Pillaging the powers

Perhaps the most significant of all these texts comes in Paul's letter to the Colossians.

> When you were dead in your sins and in the uncircumcision of your sinful nature, God made you alive with Christ. He forgave us all our sins, having cancelled the written code, with its regulations, that was against us and that stood opposed to us; he took it away, nailing it to the cross. And having disarmed the powers and authorities, he made a public spectacle of them, triumphing over them by the cross (Col. 2:13-15).

It is particularly important to follow the progression of thought in the text. First, Paul points out how the Colossians had been spiritually dead because of their sins. However, God made them alive in an act which is clearly related to the forgiveness of their sins: if sin brought death, then the pardon of sin led to life. Paul then uses an illustration to explain how that forgiveness was made possible. The word translated in the New International Version as *written code* is the Greek term *cheirographon.* In Paul's time it was often used to refer to a written statement of debt – an IOU – which somebody might sign when he or she took out a loan, and which would then be a witness against them until the debt was paid off. Paul represents sin in those terms: the 'written code' is a statement of human indebtedness in relation to God, and one that is *against us* and *stands opposed to us.* However, God has dealt with it by taking it away – literally, by taking it *out of the midst* – and himself nailing it to the cross. In other words, by his substitutionary death the Lord Jesus Christ has paid the debt on behalf of those who belong to him, and so it no longer has any force.

Paul then continues with his reference to the disarming of *the powers and authorities,* and Christ's triumphal procession in which – rather like the triumphal parade of a victorious Roman general – they are paraded as defeated enemy captives. The connection of this last idea to what Paul has been saying about sin and pardon may not be immediately obvious: why should he conclude his explanation of the believer's liberation from the debt of sin (13-14), with a sentence about the defeat of the spiritual powers of darkness (15)? The obvious reason is that there is a logical progression here, and that the two ideas are intrinsically related. What Paul seems to be saying is that God has pardoned the sin of his people through the sacrificial death of his Son, and by so doing has deprived the evil supernatural powers, including Satan himself, of what had given them their power over those people. It is as if it was the powers who held the *cheirographon* – the statement of debt – in their own hands, but God has taken it from them by settling it himself. This coincides with the idea found quite frequently elsewhere in the Bible that Satan is the accuser: he accuses Job (Job 1:9-11; 2:4-5), Joshua the priest (Zech. 3:1), and "our brothers . . . day and night" (Rev. 12:10). With the removal of the debt of sin, the basis of accusation has been once and for all removed, and the *powers and authorities* are rendered helpless – they are dispossessed of their power over those human beings who have experienced God's grace in forgiveness.

Some important implications flow from the text. First, it suggests very clearly that the power that Satan and the forces of darkness exercise over men and women is based on human sin. It is not a legitimate authority that Satan possesses as *prince of this world* he has no legal rights over the human race – but one that he has usurped. He maintains it as a parasite – like a leech that attaches itself to another living being and survives by sucking the lifeblood from its 'host'. In a similar way, Satan's power over men and women is dependent on the sin to which he tempts them, and by which he destroys them. It is for this reason that he is accuser: he accuses of sin because it is sin that gives him power, and his power is broken when sin is dealt with on the cross.

This in turn means that the central problem of men and women is not Satan and demons, but their own sin. Satan is, of course, a problem to humanity, and his activity hugely aggravates their situation, but his power is derivative and secondary. It is broken at the very moment that they are forgiven and the power of sin is shattered. The gospel of Jesus Christ is therefore always, first of all, a gospel of liberation from sin and its consequences, one of those consequences being enslavement to Satan. Moreover, this explains the mystery we noted above, how it can be that the death of Jesus brings about his victory over Satan. The reason is that by dealing with sin his death has removed the basis of Satan's power. That in turn explains why – both in the desert and later through the words of Peter – Satan sought to turn Jesus aside from the path of suffering and of the cross.

Preaching to the prisoners

One passage in Peter's first epistle may suggest that he understood the impact of Jesus' death on Satan in very much the same way as Paul.

> For Christ died for sins once for all, the righteous for the unrighteous, to bring you to God. He was put to death in the body but made alive by the Spirit, through whom also he went and preached to the spirits in prison who disobeyed long ago when God waited patiently in the days of Noah while the ark was being built (1 Pet. 3:18-20).

This is one of the most difficult passages of the Bible: "a more wonderful saying and a darker text than almost any in the New Testament" wrote Martin Luther.[3] It would be beyond our scope to go into the many interpretations that have been proposed: the text has always been a battlefield of interpretation. However, critical issues to consider are the identity of the spirits mentioned, and the time and nature of Christ's proclamation. What follows is an interpretation that

---

[3]In A. Hanson, 'Salvation Proclaimed: I. 1 Peter 3:18-22', in *ExpT 93* (1981-2), 100.

seeks to make sense of the passage in its context, and indeed in the context of the Scriptures as a whole.[4]

First, the spirits are not those of deceased human beings, but rather beings which were *created* as spirits – in other words they are demons, or fallen angels. In the New Testament the simple expression, *the spirits*, invariably refers to supernatural beings, unless there is something that clearly indicates that the spirits of dead human beings are intended. Moreover, there is no precedent in the Old Testament or ancient Jewish literature for the idea of *human* spirits in prison, whereas the notion of an imprisonment of fallen angels is well known in Jewish apocalyptic writings and elsewhere in the New Testament. In this case, therefore, these are best understood as disobedient spirits – fallen angels who have corrupted themselves in rebellion.

Secondly, the time of the proclamation is after Jesus' resurrection. According to verse 18, at the time of the proclamation Christ had been made alive – resurrected – in the sphere of the Spirit, after having been put to death in the natural realm. The contrast is not between a physical part of him and a spiritual part, but between two spheres of existence, between his previous earthly existence and his new resurrection life.

Third, the action that he undertakes is one of declaration. The verb that is translated as *preach* is often used of proclamation in an evangelistic sense, but it is not limited to that meaning and has a wider range. As the Bible never speaks

---

[4]For a more detailed discussion see R. T. France, 'Exegesis in Practice: Two Examples', in I. H. Marshall (ed.), *New Testament Interpretation* (Exeter: Paternoster Press, 1977), 252-279.

of the proclamation of an evangelistic message of grace and mercy to the spiritual powers of darkness, this communication to angels in prison can scarcely be understood as evangelistic in purpose. In the light of verse 22, where Christ is said to be enthroned "with angels, authorities and powers in submission to him", it seems most reasonable to understand the proclamation as an announcement to these spirits of his victory over them, and therefore of their defeat. The words do not, of course, necessarily refer to a literal visiting of the place of their imprisonment, but rather to the fact that the news of his redemptive work and of the consequent defeat of hostile spiritual powers has echoed throughout the cosmos.

The interpretation makes good sense in the context of the book as a whole. In this section of the letter, Peter has been particularly dealing with the trials that his readers are facing because of the fact that they are Christians. What he is saying in this text is that those very hostile spirits – including Satan himself (1 Pet. 5:8) – who stand behind the persecutors and seek to destroy the church of Christ, have already been defeated, and Christ reigns over them even now. Believers need not fear for their own eternal security: the one who saved them is also the conqueror of their foes, and he can assure their perseverance and final victory.

There is one more crucial point. Before referring to Christ's proclamation to the spirits, Peter has given a brilliantly concise explanation of his atoning death: "For Christ died for sins once for all, the righteous for the unrighteous, to bring you to God" (3:18). The flow of thought suggests that it is his death "for sins" that is the basis of that victory over the spirits which he goes on to proclaim to them. In other words, the flow of Peter's argument echoes quite closely that of Paul in Colossians 2:13-15: the spirits are parasites on sin and so, because Christ has died for sins "once for all", the basis of their power is removed and the proclamation of their defeat is made to them. Peter is clearly using language and imagery different to that employed by Paul in Colossians 2, but he is saying the same thing.

Driving out the dragon

In his description of "war in heaven" and its aftermath, the author of Revelation, probably the apostle John, uses imagery that is quite different from that of both Paul and Peter in the passages just discussed. Nevertheless, his imagery communicates essentially the same truth – that Christ has defeated Satan and the powers of darkness by dealing with human sin.

> And there was war in heaven. Michael and his angels fought against the dragon, and the dragon and his angels fought back. But he was not strong enough, and they lost their place in heaven. The great dragon was hurled down – that ancient serpent called the devil, or Satan, who leads the whole world astray. He was hurled to the earth, and his angels with him. Then I heard a loud voice in heaven say: "Now have come the salvation and the power and the kingdom of our God, and the authority of his Christ. For the accuser of our brothers, who accuses them before our God day and night, has been hurled down. They overcame him by the blood of the Lamb and by the word of their testimony; they did not love their lives so much as to shrink from death" (Rev. 12:7-11).

The critical factor in understanding the passage is to get behind the apocalyptic imagery in order to determine what exactly John means by it. In a literal sense, he speaks of the expulsion of Satan from heaven in a great cosmic battle, but what does that mean, and when did the battle take place? There are two principal interpretive keys.

First, the war in heaven and the resulting defeat of Satan follow the brief – and again very symbolic – narrative of the coming of Christ in the first section of the chapter. In those verses (12:1-6) a child (the Messiah) is born from among the people of God, who are represented by the woman. Meanwhile Satan (the dragon) stands ready to destroy the child at the very moment of birth. However, the ascension of the child to heaven – "And her child was snatched up to God and to his throne" (12:5) – signifies the frustration of the dragon's purposes, and the fulfillment of the child's mission, which implicitly includes his death and resurrection and all that they mean. In the flow of the narrative, therefore, it is as a result of the accomplishment of the Messiah's mission that war in heaven takes place, and the dragon and his army are expelled. Satan loses his place because of the incarnation of Christ and all that results from that.

Second, John emphasizes the fact that it is *as the accuser* of believers that Satan is defeated and hurled down: "the accuser of our brothers, who accuses them before our God day and night, has been hurled down" (Rev. 12:10). Therefore, what the apocalyptic imagery of Satan's ejection from heaven means in *literal* terms is that he is no longer able to accuse of sin those who now belong to Christ.

Putting these two central points together, John is saying that Christ's coming into the world and the accomplishment of his mission there has deprived Satan of the basis on which he can accuse. This must imply an understanding of the impact of the cross on Satan which is identical to that in Colossians 2 and 1 Peter 3. By the fulfilment of his mission through death and resurrection, Christ has dealt with the problem of sin; *in consequence* the devil is deprived of the basis on which he can accuse those – *our brothers* – who belong to Christ, and has thereby lost his power over them. The final verse in the section confirms this. The *brothers* have now overcome Satan. They are freed from the bondage that he formerly imposed on them, and they have done that, first of all, "by the blood of the lamb" – which in the context of the whole book undoubtedly refers to Jesus' sacrificial death for sins (Rev. 1:5; 5:9; 7:14).

This understanding of the text also explains why it is Michael and not Christ who drives Satan from heaven. In the context of John's symbolism, the primary victory – that over sin – is achieved by Christ on the cross; Satan's expulsion from heaven is a *secondary* consequence but it takes place at the same time as Christ's death and so, in terms of the narrative, it occurs when he is still on earth. As one commentator says, "Because he is part of the earthly reality, He [Christ] is not part of the heavenly symbolism."[5]

Destroying the devil

Finally, the author of the epistle to the Hebrews also refers very briefly to the impact of the cross of Christ on Satan.

---

[5]G.B. Caird, 'On Deciphering the Book of Revelation', in *ExpT 74* (1962- 3), 13.

> Since the children have flesh and blood, he too shared
> in their humanity so that by his death he might destroy
> him who holds the power of death – that is, the devil –
> and free those who all their lives were held in slavery
> by their fear of death (Heb. 2:14- 15).

The text indicates that the reason Jesus took human nature
was that he should die, and the purpose of his death is
identified here as the *destruction* of Satan. It is a striking
statement because almost everywhere else in Hebrews,
Christ's death is understood as an atonement for sins; this text
seems to run counter to the dominant theme of the book.
However, it can nevertheless, be understood in a way that is
compatible with the epistle's primary atonement perspective.
In the New Testament, death is the result of sin and, while the
author of Hebrews does not explicitly make that connection,
it is nevertheless implicit throughout the book since Christ
himself died on account of the sins of others (Hebrews 9:14,
15, 26, 28). When the devil is called "him who holds the
power of death," the death referred to is that which is also
the penalty of sin. In other words, he may indeed "hold the
power of death," but the reason that people die at all is
not primarily because of him but rather because they are
sinners and are therefore subject to God's own judgement on
sin. Accordingly, reflecting the epistle's dominant emphasis
on the atoning value of the cross, by removing sins Christ
deals with the root cause of human death – and in so doing
he strikes "the power of death," namely sin – from Satan's
hand. The death which Satan wielded as a weapon, is nullified
because the power of sin itself is cancelled out at the cross.
To put this another way, it is not that Jesus *both* removed

sins *and* destroyed Satan's power, but that Satan's power is shattered specifically by Jesus' sin-bearing death. This in turn means that redeemed humanity is delivered from fear of death (2:15). Clearly this does not imply that the physical reality of death no longer occurs, but rather that it has been rendered powerless; the very thing that made it terrifying, namely sin and the judgement of God that must necessarily follow, has been dealt with. Death has therefore become ineffectual as the instrument of Satan's tyranny.

Thus, the text implies that Satan exploits sin to cause death, just as he sought to do in Eden. As in the passages considered above, he feeds on human sin for the exercise of his power – the power, as always, of the destroyer and murderer. While Christ's death can be explained as the instrument of Satan's 'destruction', the foundation of Satan's power over fallen men and women is actually removed by dealing with sin. It is this that explains the brevity of the reference to Satan in Hebrews.

It is, of course, possible to contest the interpretation of any of the four texts discussed above. What is striking, however, is that although they use very different images, Peter, Paul, John and the unknown writer of Hebrews, all seem to be saying the same thing. On the cross Christ died to make atonement for the sins of men and women, to bring about their forgiveness, and thereby to restore them to the Father. By so doing he also broke the power of Satan who exploits human sin to keep lost humanity in slavery to himself. The defeat of the parasitic powers of evil is, therefore, a consequence of the much greater victory over sin, with which the New Testament writers are far more concerned.

Enthronement

One of the most important and widespread affirmations in the New Testament is the fact that Jesus Christ, having died on the cross, has now risen from the dead and ascended into heaven, and is seated at the right hand of God. Every strand of the New Testament declares that he is Lord of heaven and earth, and that the whole cosmos is subject to him (for example, Matt. 28:18-20; Acts 2:33; Eph. 1:20-22; Phil. 2:9-11; Heb. 1:3; 1 Pet. 3:22; Rev. 5:6). When he met the disciples in Galilee just before his return to the Father, he declared, "All authority on heaven and on earth has been given to me" (Matt. 28:18). Moreover, the one Old Testament verse that is quoted or alluded to in the New Testament more than any other (in fact 33 times) is Psalm 110:1: "The LORD says to my Lord: 'Sit at my right hand until I make your enemies a footstool for your feet'." It was this text that Peter quoted on the day of Pentecost to explain the coming of the Spirit. The Spirit had been poured out by the Lord Jesus, which was proof that Jesus was exalted to the right hand of God, from whom he had received the Spirit (Acts 2:33-34). It is, moreover, especially significant that the psalm not only refers to his exaltation to the place of supreme power, but also to the subduing of his enemies. This made it particularly relevant for New Testament writers as they reflected on his conflict with the powers of evil.

Jesus' enthronement does not, of course, add anything to God's sovereignty. God is always the ruler of heaven and earth, and Satan is – and has always been – subject to the divine government. What is different now is the fact that Jesus Christ, as the one through whom salvation is accomplished, has been given the place of absolute power in order to bring to fulfilment the salvation of his people, and to complete the final conquest of his enemies (1 Cor. 15:24-26). On the cross he died to save his people; now, on the throne, he reigns to bring about the completion of their salvation.

There are two very important implications of this. First, as he reigns Christ assures the growth of the church. This is especially evident in the final commission he gave to his disciples at the end of Matthew: "All authority in heaven and on earth has been given to me. Therefore go and make disciples of all nations. . ." (Matt. 28:18-19). There is a clear causal link in the text between his universal reign and the making of disciples: the king's authority gives his messengers the right to go to every part of his realm and summon men and women to acknowledge him as Lord through baptism in the name of the triune God. Furthermore, since Jesus has authority in heaven – that is, in the spiritual realm – as well as on earth, it gives the disciples confidence to carry out their commission in the face of hostility from Satan, *the prince of this world*, who would try by every means to hinder the fulfilment of their mission. This also echoes somewhat Jesus' words to his disciples in Luke 10:19: "I have given you authority to trample on snakes and scorpions and to overcome all the power of the enemy." Through his death, resurrection and exaltation, Jesus Christ now rules the universe, building his church, and Satan cannot prevent him doing so. Whereas previously the knowledge of the true God had been more or less limited to the people of Israel, since Jesus' exaltation the gospel has penetrated to almost every corner of the earth. He has expelled Satan (John 12:31-32) in such a way that the messengers of the gospel can advance with the gospel, knowing that their

Lord will redeem a people for himself. Despite all the trials they may have to endure, this is the root of the confidence that they have as ambassadors of Christ: as sovereign Lord over all, Christ *will* build his church.

For it remains the case that Satan attacks the church, and especially those who bring good news. In this context Christ's exaltation is, secondly, the basis of his people's assurance that they will survive whatever attacks the devil may launch against them. This is especially clear in Paul's words of encouragement to the Ephesians. Towards the end of the first chapter of his epistle he reminds them that Christ has been exalted over every evil spiritual power:

> [God] seated him at his right hand in the heavenly realms, far above all rule and authority, power and dominion, and every title that can be given, not only in the present age but also in the one to come. And God placed all things under his feet (Eph. 1:20-22).

The reference to "every title that can be given" is intended to assure the Ephesian believers that there is absolutely no power spiritual or otherwise, known to them or unknown, which is not subject to Christ's rule. In the next chapter, however, Paul points out that they, the believers, are themselves seated with him in glory:

> [God] made us alive with Christ even when we were dead in transgressions – it is by grace you have been saved. And God raised us up with Christ and seated us with him in the heavenly realms in Christ Jesus (Eph. 2:5-6).

The point is that the Christian's security is as solid as Christ's supreme authority; in a spiritual sense nothing can touch the child of God, because he is now, already, "in Christ" and so has been raised with Christ to God's right hand. These words in this context are extremely significant. The Ephesian Christians lived in one of the great centres of magic of the first-century Roman world, and would have been deeply conscious of the menace that came from the powers of darkness. It is for this reason that Paul stresses Christ's victory and present reign. He wants them to understand that because they are in Christ the forces of evil – including Satan, demons, sorcerers, curses – have no power over them except such as Christ himself may allow for their good. Their lives are in his hands, and their salvation is absolutely and eternally safe. Jesus has a name – an authority – that far surpasses that of any and every other power.

Return

In the Old Testament Isaiah looked forward to the final defeat of every enemy of God, including supernatural foes:

> In that day the LORD will punish the powers in the heavens above and the kings on the earth below. They will be herded together like prisoners bound in a dungeon; they will be shut up in prison and be punished after many days. . . In that day, the LORD will punish with his sword, his fierce, great and powerful sword, Leviathan the gliding serpent, Leviathan the coiling serpent; he will slay the monster of the sea (24:21-22 and 27:1).

The reference to the slaughter of Leviathan evokes the idea of the great supernatural adversary of God elsewhere identified as Satan. Moreover, in 24:21, Isaiah implies that human kings are allied with "the powers in the heavens above" in a conspiracy against God that will finally be crushed.

Paul, too, refers to the final decisive judgement of the powers of evil, but it is now clear that it is the Lord Jesus Christ himself who will carry it out:

> Then the end will come, when he hands over the kingdom to God the Father after he has destroyed all dominion, authority and power. For he must reign until he has put all his enemies under his feet (1 Cor. 15:24-5).

The Saviour's final act in his conflict with Satan will take place at his return, when he will bring about Satan's final judgement and condemnation. It will not this time be a victory carried out through suffering on a cross, but he will return in the power of God to crush by overwhelming power, and once for all, everything that sets itself up against the reign of God. Towards the end of Revelation, John stresses the awesome, transcendent nature of the final victory in words that echo those of Isaiah, which we have just quoted:

> But fire came down from heaven and devoured them.
> And the devil, who deceived them, was thrown into the
> lake of burning sulphur (20:9-10).

And so the new heaven and new earth come, which contain no sea (Rev. 21:1). In Ancient Near Eastern mythology, the sea was seen as a primal force of chaos and evil. Such notions are categorically excluded by the biblical doctrine of creation which demythologises the sea and subjects it – along with every other created thing – to God's sovereign rule. Nevertheless, the symbolism of the 'demonic sea' is sometimes used in the Bible to communicate truth, and that is happening in this text. Hence the affirmation, "and there was no longer any sea", means that every conceivable evil or source of evil is definitively and forever banished from the new creation: the Lamb's victory over Satan and all his army is complete.

Conclusion

In reflecting on the power of Satan and his forces, and the conflict that believers have with them, no truth is more important than the victory that Christ accomplishes over all the powers of evil. Satan is not only a creature made by God and subject always to his sovereign rule, but he is also a defeated and literally hopeless rebel. The victory of Christ is a complex one that takes place in several stages, and it is not yet finalized. Nevertheless, the crucial moment, the decisive combat, took place at the cross where Jesus broke the power of the evil one over lost human beings, and did so by bearing their sins in his sacrificial death. As a result believers participate already in the triumph that Christ has won for them: they have even now overcome the dragon "by the blood of the lamb" (Rev. 12:11). Yet they must fight. It is to that paradox – victory and conflict – that we turn now.

Questions for further reflection

1. In what ways do the temptations we face resemble those Jesus experienced in the wilderness?

2. Do demons still 'possess' people where you live? If they do, should believers still cast them out? And if so, how should they do it?

3. 'Now is the time for judgment on this world; now the prince of this world will be driven out' (Jn. 12:31). In what sense or senses has Satan been driven out?

4. If fear of spiritual powers is strong within a people's culture, should that affect the way in which the gospel is communicated to them?

5. What encouragement should believers draw from Jesus' words, 'I have given you authority to trample on snakes and scorpions and to overcome all the power of the enemy; nothing will harm you'?

6. Why are there parts of the world where the gospel has still not penetrated after 2000 years? What should be done about it?

CHAPTER 5

SALVATION AND STRUGGLE

But now, in this valley of HUMILIATION, poor CHRISTIAN was
hard put to it; for he had gone but a little way, before he espied
a foul fiend coming over the field to meet him: his name is
APOLLYON. Then did CHRISTIAN begin to be afraid, and to
cast in his mind whether to go back or to stand his ground. But
he considered again, that he had no armour for his back, and
therefore thought that to turn the back to him might give him
greater advantage, with ease to pierce him with his darts: therefore
he resolved to venture and stand his ground: for, thought he, had
I no more in mine eye than the saving of my life, 'twould be the
best way to stand.

So he went on, and APOLLYON met him …

Then APOLLYON straddled quite over the whole breadth of
the way, and said, I am void of fear in this matter; prepare thyself
to die; for I swear by my infernal den that thou shalt go no further:
here will I spill thy soul.

And with that he threw a flaming dart at his breast; but
CHRISTIAN had a shield in his hand, with which he caught it, and
so prevented the danger of that.

Then did CHRISTIAN draw, for he saw 'twas time to bestir him; and APOLLYON as fast made at him, throwing darts as thick as hail; by the which, notwithstanding all that CHRISTIAN could do to avoid it, APOLLYON wounded him in his head, his hand, and foot. This made CHRISTIAN give a little back: Apollyon, therefore, followed his work amain, and CHRISTIAN again took courage, and resisted as manfully as he could. This sore combat lasted for above half a day, even till CHRISTIAN was almost quite spent: for you must know, that CHRISTIAN, by reason of his wounds, must needs grow weaker and weaker.

Then APOLLYON, espying his opportunity, began to gather up close to CHRISTIAN, and wrestling with him, gave him a dreadful fall; and with that CHRISTIAN'S sword flew out of his hand. Then said APOLLYON, I am sure of thee now: and with that he had almost prest him to death, so that CHRISTIAN began to despair of life. But, as GOD would have it, while APOLLYON was fetching of his last blow, thereby to make a full end of this good man, CHRISTIAN nimbly reached out his hand for his sword, and caught it, saying, "Rejoice not against me, O mine enemy: when I fall, I shall arise;" and with that gave him a deadly thrust, which made him give back as one that had received his mortal wound. CHRISTIAN perceiving that made at him again, saying, "Nay, in all these things we are more than conquerors, through him that loved us;" and with that APOLLYON spread forth his dragon's wings and sped him away, that CHRISTIAN saw him no more.

In this combat no man can imagine, unless he had seen and heard, as I did, what yelling and hideous roaring APOLLYON made all the time of the fight; he spake like a dragon: and, on the other side, what sighs and groans burst from CHRISTIAN'S heart. I never saw him all the while give so much as one pleasant look, till he perceived he had wounded APOLLYON with his two edged sword; then indeed he did smile and look upward! but 'twas the dreadfullest fight that ever I saw.

So when the battle was over, CHRISTIAN said, I will here give thanks to him that hath delivered me out of the mouth of the lion, to him that did help me against APOLLYON. And so he did …[1]

The Christian is a person who has been redeemed. He or she has been forgiven, born again, and delivered from Satan's power by the work that God has accomplished through Christ, and the implications of this multiple liberation are rich and varied. This fundamental truth needs to be grasped before moving on to consider the spiritual warfare in which Christians are involved. For it means that this warfare takes place – and must be understood – in the context of the victory *already* gained by Christ. Believers face a struggle with the world, the flesh and the devil. However, it is not a struggle that determines whether they will be finally saved or lost. Rather, it is a struggle that takes place because they have *already* been saved through the death and resurrection of Jesus Christ. Moreover, it is one in which they have the assurance of his constant presence and of the indwelling power of the Holy Spirit in their lives to guide and sustain them.

Nevertheless, there *is* a spiritual warfare that begins with redemption, and it is intense. Christians experience spiritual conflict in a way that was not true of their pre-conversion experience. However, the warfare that they experience is sharply distinct from the way in which African traditional

---

[1] J. Bunyan, *Pilgrim's Progress*, (London: L. B. Seeley, 1801), 101-111.

religion has tended to perceive the threat that spirits may present to human beings.

A triple liberation – and a triple warfare

Why does the Christian face conflict with the powers of darkness? In response, one must understand the situation of the unbeliever in the light of Paul's explanation in Ephesians 2:1-2. He or she lives in a condition of tripartite slavery – to sin, to the world, and to Satan:

> . . . you were dead in your transgressions and sins [*slavery to sin*]. . . you followed the ways of this world [*slavery to the world*] and of the ruler of the kingdom of the air, the spirit who is now at work in those who are disobedient [*slavery to Satan*]. All of us also lived among them at one time [*slavery to the world*], gratifying the cravings of our sinful nature and following its desires and thoughts [*slavery to sin*].

In these few phrases, Paul summarises the condition of every unredeemed human being. However, God has totally transformed the situation of those who have come to faith in Christ. In all three areas where they were previously enslaved, they have now been freed. It is the very fact of their liberation which means that they now face conflict as the forces from which they have been freed try to recover what they have lost. Thus, believers are confronted by a sustained counter-attack on the part of Satan, the world and the remnants of sin in their own hearts.

First of all, the believer is freed from the domination of the old sinful nature: "you have been set free from sin" (Rom 6:18, 22). Christians are no longer slaves of sin and subject to its condemnation, but they have become sons of God who are liberated from both its power and its penalty.

However, they still experience the 'remains' of sin in their lives, enticing them to do evil and challenging the reality of their repentance. The result is an ongoing battle. While Paul can say unambiguously that the Roman believers had been freed from sin, he still urges them, "do not let sin reign in your mortal body so that you obey its evil desires" (Rom. 6:12). The Spirit's work in their lives now *enables* them to resist the domination of sin, which was not the case before. They do not have to continue to be what they once were, for sin's mastery over them is broken. This involves a constant conflict against tendencies that have not been finally and totally rooted out. Consequently, a consistent testimony of true believers through the ages has been that their biggest spiritual problem is with themselves and their own hearts.

Redemption also means freedom from the 'world'. Jesus told his disciples, "you do not belong to the world, but I have chosen you out of the world" (John 15:19). Similarly, Peter tells his readers that they are now strangers in the world, and should *live* as strangers (1 Pet. 1:1, 17; 2:11). But what does that mean? When the New Testament speaks of the "world" in this sense, it means human society united in its rebellion against God. As such, humanity shares a sinful mindset, which John calls elsewhere "the cravings of sinful man, the lust of his eyes and the boasting of what he has and does" (1 John 2:16). The notion of the "world" in this sense of spiritual rebellion focuses primarily on a set of values, attitudes and dispositions which tend to characterize all fallen human beings. It is often expressed through culture and worldview, but at heart it is about rebellious human society asserting its autonomy over against its creator and pursuing its own distorted desires. As a result of being redeemed from the world, believers no longer belong to it in that sense. They can experience freedom from its control, and their lives and way of thinking will be different from those that characterize the societies they live in.

However, as a result they now face conflict with the *world*, and there are at least two dimensions to it. First, physically they still live in the world, although they have become *foreigners* and *pilgrims* whose real citizenship belongs elsewhere (Heb. 13:14). They are under a constant moral and spiritual pressure to conform to its norms and expectations, its thinking and behaviour: the world presses in on them remorselessly, and seeks to squeeze them into its mould. In order to withstand that pressure they must intentionally determine no longer to live under the power of the world – just as they determine no longer to live under the domination of sin. They must refuse to love it or anything in it (1 John 2:15). In order to live out such a life of non-conformity to the world that surrounds them, they must nurture minds that are transformed (Rom. 12:2): their thinking needs more and more to be set free from the values and priorities held by those around them.

Secondly, they must also expect to experience active hostility from the world, for it hates them just as it hated their Saviour, and wants to reclaim them (John 16:33). There is opposition to the difference manifested in their lives, and to their participation now in the mission of God. As he revisited churches founded during his first missionary journey, this was the theme of Paul's teaching to the new believers: "We must go through many hardships to enter the kingdom of God" (Acts 14:22). This is evident in a wide range of forms. It may be religious persecution in the name of Islam or some other religion, including secular religions like Marxism. In postmodern Western cultures, it can take the form of a strident and abusive hostility – in the name of pluralism, relativism and so-called *tolerance* – to the idea that Jesus Christ is the only Saviour. This is strikingly similar to the grounds of opposition to Christianity in the earliest centuries.

Finally, Christians are redeemed from the power of Satan. As we have seen, the unbelieving world lies under his control (1 John 5:19), and he is its "prince" and "god" (John 12:31; 14:30; 16:11; 2 Cor. 4:4). However, God has broken Satan's power through Christ's death, which brings freedom from the guilt and power of sin for his people, and simultaneously results in their liberation from Satan's tyranny. This is strikingly expressed in Paul's words to the Colossians, where again the flow of thought is important: "he has rescued us from the dominion of darkness and brought us into the kingdom of the Son he loves, in whom we have redemption, the forgiveness of sins" (Col. 1:13-14). Paul is saying that believers have been rescued from the powers of darkness, including Satan. This redemption has taken place in Christ, but the redemption is itself to be defined in terms of the forgiveness of sins. Again, the assumption is that human beings are subject to Satan because of their sins; when their sins are dealt with they are freed from Satan's power. And the opening words of Galatians make a simple point: ". . . the Lord Jesus Christ, who gave himself for our sins to rescue us from *the present evil age,* according to the will of our God and

Father" (Gal. 1:3-4). It was by giving himself for sins that Jesus rescued men and women from the present evil age – that is, the world, which is under Satan's control.

Nevertheless, Satan remains the arch-adversary of God and aims to destroy all God's work. For believers, the result yet again is conflict, which takes two main forms. First, Satan pursues the church to try to destroy those who have been rescued from his grasp. The writer of Revelation indicates the bitterness and violence of this pursuit (Rev. 12:13-17), which in his narrative took two primary forms: political – the beast from the sea, and religious – the beast from the earth (Rev. 13). Believers are exposed to his malice in many forms, including temptation to all the various expressions of sin, which are intended to seduce them, or violence, whose purpose is to intimidate them into submission. As they faced persecution on account of their faith, Peter warned his Christian readers to beware of Satan who was the inspiration of the persecutors: "your enemy the devil prowls round like a roaring lion seeking for someone to devour" (1 Pet. 5:8). However, the fact that they experienced Satan's hostility was not a cause for doubting their Christian experience, but rather evidence of its reality. Second, Satan also uses every means possible to halt the church's mission and the proclamation of the gospel. Paul recognized Satan's hostile influence when he could not get back to the church at Thessalonica, despite repeated efforts to do so: "For we wanted to come to you – certainly I, Paul, did, again and again – but Satan stopped us" (1 Thess. 2:18). Or again, when the magician Elymas opposed his preaching at Paphos, Paul stated, "you are a child of the devil" (Acts 13:10).

Spiritual warfare is the conflict Christians and churches must wage with remaining sin, with the world and with the devil, *because* they are Christians and churches. It is a conflict that they would not know if God himself had not redeemed them. In that sense, it is an evidence of their salvation so that, in a paradoxical way, they may actually take heart from it.

Dynamics of warfare

The warfare that Christians face takes many forms and there are, to begin with, a number of general features that characterize it.

It is *only Christians* who experience spiritual warfare in this sense, for only they are the object of attack by those forces that are opposed to God. It comes about due to the overlap of two ages – what is sometimes referred to as eschatological tension. This means that, on the one hand, the reign of God and the salvation it brings have already broken into the present age of darkness, to liberate people for God. They are freed from bondage to sin, the world and the devil, and they belong now to the kingdom of God's Son – the future age. They already have eternal life and the Holy Spirit; they have already experienced judgement and been acquitted – justified – in Christ; and they are already reconciled with God, adopted into his family, and seated with Christ in heavenly realms. However, *at the same time* those three evil realities – world, flesh and devil – although defeated, remain active: the present age of darkness continues and, because Christians still live on earth, they face its constant hostility. Therefore, they have *already* been saved, but they are *not yet* definitively removed from the presence of evil powers, which continue to assault them. They experience a double reality: they have received the eternal life of the age to come, but for the moment they must still do battle with the powers of this present fallen age that seek to undermine and even to destroy that life.

The situation is like that which sometimes occurs in human warfare, when an enemy has been decisively defeated in a crucial battle and destruction is certain, but he struggles on hopelessly and bitterly tries to inflict damage.

> The decisive battle in a war may already have occurred in a relatively early stage of the war, and yet the war still continues. Although the decisive effect of the battle is perhaps not recognized by all, it nevertheless already means victory. But the war must still be carried on for an undefined time, until 'Victory Day'.[2]

So it is with Satan. As he contemplates the church of Christ and what her existence means for his own final destiny, he "is filled with fury, because he knows that his time is short" (Rev. 12:12). However, far from surrendering and giving up the fight, he makes war on her – futilely but nevertheless venomously.

It is a conflict which arises from two fundamental facts: on the one hand there is the *redemption* that Christians have received, and on the other there is the *mission* with which God has entrusted them, namely that of taking the good news of Christ and the redemption he has accomplished into the world. In this context, the three forces of Satan, sin and the world have a double objective: they fight against the believers' new life and try to kill it, and at the same time they struggle

---

[2]O. Cullmann, *Christ and Time: The Primitive Christian Conception of Time and History* (Philadelphia: Westminster, 1964), 84.

against the task that God has given them and try to stop it advancing. There is a parallel here with Satan's temptations of Jesus in the desert when he tried to undermine both Jesus' sense of identity and his fulfilment of the mission the Father had given him. Nevertheless, the two are carried out by very much the same means: a primary way of stopping mission is to discourage or seduce the people of God as they engage in it.

It is a conflict from which there is no escape, except when believers leave this present world through death, or when Christ returns. In this present age, there is no vacation from the conflict, no home leave, no ceasefire and no weekend. Nor can Christians concentrate on just one front at a time. They most often face a hostile alliance of two or even all three of their 'spiritual enemies' at once, for the three powers do not work separately but in concert. Satan exploits the world and the remains of sin in believers in order to seduce them; while due to the continuing tug of their old sinful habits, Christians continue to feel an attraction to the evil aspects of the life of the present world order.

It is a conflict in which believers bear responsibility for their own conduct. This is a critical point. Although Satan and the world are active in all of this warfare, that does not diminish the *responsibility* of individual believers for their own moral and spiritual failures. When they fall short, they cannot simply see themselves as helpless – and therefore guiltless – victims. When speaking of marriage and sexual temptation, Paul tells the Corinthians that they should not let Satan tempt them because of *their own* lack of self-control (1 Cor. 7:5). The fact that Satan tempts does not exonerate the Corinthian believers – nor Christians of any other time or place – from guilt if they should fall. When he refers to anger, Paul again says that his readers should not give the devil an opportunity (Eph. 4:26-27). He mentions some who need to repent of the false doctrine they have embraced, and so escape from "the devil's snare" (2 Tim. 2:26). By temptation and seduction, Satan exploits the sinful and corrupt tendencies that already characterize even regenerate men and women, but he cannot coerce in such a way that they simply have no choice. Nobody can ever say, 'Satan made me do it,' as to do so would be to avoid personal and group responsibility for sin. That in turn would mean denying the reality of human sin altogether, for there can be no sin where there is no responsibility for one's own actions. The concept of guilt would disappear and the substitutionary work of Christ would be unnecessary. In fact, removing human responsibility for sin would be dehumanising at a fundamental level – undermining the dignity and freedom with which human beings are endowed as those created in the very image of God, and which makes them truly human. Human beings, Christian and non-Christian alike, are never simply victims and playthings of Satan, but fully responsible for moral failure in their own lives. It is vital to understand this: ". . . each one is tempted when, *by his own evil desire*, he is dragged away and enticed" (James 1:14).

It is a conflict that rages across the whole range of the Christian's life – home, work, church and so on. There has sometimes been a tendency to reserve the expression, 'spiritual warfare', for a somewhat constricted area of Christian experience concerned especially with such matters as demonic possession and deliverance, witchcraft and sorcery. It is true that spiritual warfare may take such forms, but it is essential to recognize that it is far wider than they are, and concerns every area in which the world, the flesh and the devil seek to draw believers away from Christ and hinder their testimony. It is dangerously unbalanced to understand spiritual warfare simply in terms of liberating victims of possession or somehow dealing with witches and sorcerers. Failure to recognize the breadth of the conflict will mean failure to be appropriately "self- controlled and alert" in the face of all the ways in which the devil seeks to "devour" the people of God (1 Pet. 5:8).

Finally, it is a conflict in which the *victory is already won*, and believers may count on the resources of God as they face the foe. It is imperative to keep returning to these foundational truths, for a proper understanding of the *context* of the battle will determine the way in which Christians confront it. They fight against sin, the world and Satan with the strength that God himself gives them through his Spirit, and they are sure of the final outcome for Christ has already overcome every enemy through his death and resurrection. Through believing in him, believers are united with him in his death, resurrection and victory, and have access to the strength that he supplies.

It is particularly important to recognize this in reflecting on Satan's attacks. Christians should not regard him as a foe with strength equal to that of God, and so perhaps suppose that the final result of their conflict is uncertain. On the contrary, Satan is a creature made by God, and cannot *at any point* act outside of the sovereign rule of the Creator. Moreover, he has been overcome through the cross and resurrection of Christ, and he fights on hopelessly as he awaits

the final return of Christ and the definitive destruction of his
own power (Rev. 12:12). It is true that Satan is much stronger
than human beings, and that Christians cannot defeat him in
their own strength alone. He is, however, infinitely weaker
than God. It is God who made him, defeated him, and will
finally overcome him and eliminate his power forever; and it
is the same almighty God who equips his people so that they
can "stand" against the attacks of their enemy, "strong in the
Lord and in his mighty power" (Eph. 6:10). In Christ they are
already "in all these things . . . more than conquerors" (Rom.
8:37). Therefore, the church fights – and individual believers
must fight – but they do so in God's own strength and are
confident of ultimate victory because Christ has already won
it. All that is said in the remaining paragraphs of this chapter
must be understood from this perspective.

Battlefields

In war, generals try to choose the battlefield that will be
most favourable to them. In spiritual warfare, Satan similarly
selects with care the areas where he will fight God's people,
and they need to make sure they are ready. They may not
themselves be able to choose the ground on which they fight,
but they can be alert, recognising the evil shrewdness of their
enemy. Paul wrote to the Corinthians, "we are not unaware
of his schemes" (2 Cor. 2:11), and clearly expected them to
understand something of the strategy and tactics Satan uses
in his warfare. The problem is that too often Christians are
in fact unaware of Satan's schemes – and even perhaps of the
reality of spiritual conflict itself – and, in their naivety, they
are caught unprepared when he attacks them, and are more

likely to succumb. Meanwhile, Satan identifies areas in which Christians and churches are especially weak, and strikes at those points.

Another danger is evident when believers seriously misunderstand the nature of the battle by interpreting it in terms of their own misguided cultural or theological preconceptions. This happens, for example, when they attribute their own sins to evil spirits, and so respond to moral failure not by repentance but by casting out some supposed 'spirit of anger' or 'spirit of adultery'. It may also happen when, in the face of trials and difficulties, they pursue the witches or sorcerers supposedly responsible and try to 'cleanse' them with 'holy water' or some other purification ritual. Such misunderstandings stem from a failure to allow the Bible to shape their understanding of the invisible world and the threat that it poses, and the result is a reversion to traditional ways of thinking and acting, in substance if not always in form.

It is, therefore, very important to identify accurately the battlefields that Satan is most likely to choose and to be ready when he strikes, while recognising also that he may well launch an attack where it is least expected. Christians are caught up in all-encompassing and total warfare and the areas where we can expect conflict cover the whole of human experience – every dimension of life and ministry. Looking at the New Testament we can identify many situations of spiritual warfare where Christians will face conflict in their lives and their service for God.

Sin

Sin is the most obvious battlefield of all. Satan wants to seduce Christians into renewed rebellion against the will of God, and so spiritual warfare is, more than anything else, about the struggle believers face every day with temptations to sin. He seeks to draw them back into the patterns of sinful behaviour which are usual in their societies, and which would therefore seem normal and acceptable to those only recently redeemed from them. For this reason, there are frequent warnings in the New Testament about the dangers of sexual sin, because the Greco-Roman Gentile world of the time was characterized by sexual laxity including fornication, adultery and homosexuality. The port of Corinth, in particular, had become a byword for sexual immorality, which explains Paul's exhortations on the matter in 1 Corinthians. He similarly counsels the Thessalonians at some length on the necessity of holiness in sexual relationships (1 Thess. 4:1-8). For African Christians, the danger may more likely be that of reversion to the powerfully influential belief structure of witchcraft and sorcery and the practices that flow from it. This might take the form of employing sorcery to advance personal self-interest or settle scores, of using traditional defences such as fetishes and amulets to ensure protection against sorcerers and witches, or of participating in witch-hunts and the witchcraft paranoia that may quickly lead to violence against those suspected of occult aggression. We return to this issue in the next section.

Temptation to sin is the pre-eminent means that Satan employs to undermine Christians' walk with God as well as the credibility of their testimony before the watching world. Clearly, the sins of Christians have a negative impact on the mission of the church. In addressing the Corinthians about the scandalous sexual behaviour of one of their members, Paul stresses the way in which moral degeneracy on the part of just one believer can infiltrate the church as a whole with dire consequences for its testimony (1 Cor. 5:1-13). The letters to the seven churches at the beginning of Revelation similarly warn against a tendency at times to tolerate sin rather than deal with it (Rev. 2:14-16, 20- 23). When they slip back into sin, Christians cease to make a difference; their lives blend once again with the pattern of the fallen world rather than confronting that world with the transforming message of Christ.

Nor is the spoiling of the church's testimony all that Satan has in mind. By luring the believer back into the old sin-controlled way of life, his ultimate ambition is to re-impose his own tyranny. It is a tyranny always based, as we have seen, on the sin of the tyrannised, and one from which believers are freed through Christ's atoning sacrifice for sins. In their brief letters Peter and Jude warned about contempt towards "celestial beings", which some godless people in the churches were displaying. Although the issue is debated, the reference to celestial beings (*doxai*) probably refers to forces of darkness (2 Pet. 2:10-11; Jude 8-10), while the meaning of the warning is a little obscure. It is quite likely, however, that the people Peter and Jude refer to scorned the possibility that their own sinful behaviour would bring them back into bondage to evil powers. They were not so much showing contempt for the *persons* of the *celestial beings*, but rather for the very real moral danger they represented. Their attitude was a presumptuous one – they thought they could sin with impunity and that, because they were redeemed, Satan could do nothing to them regardless of their behaviour. If a believer is one who has been freed from the kingdom of darkness, evidently the great goal of the ruler of darkness is to get them back – to recover the captives. A contemptuous disregard of that real possibility simply plays into his hands.

Falsehood

False belief – error and heresy – is a second battlefield on which Satan fights against the people of God. The words of Jesus Christ defining the devil's character are critically important: "not holding to the truth, for there is no truth in him. When he lies, he speaks his native language, for he is a liar and the father of lies" (John 8:44). As a liar, Satan seeks to undermine Christians' hold on truth. When he spoke of some who had parted company with the truth, Paul referred to "deceiving spirits and things taught by demons" (1 Tim. 4:1), and the New Testament documents indicate that the introduction of error among the people of God was going on from the very beginning of the church's history.

Indeed, the very first temptation, that of Adam and Eve – which might be seen as the *pattern* or *model* temptation – at its heart questioned fundamental, God-given truths. Satan flatly denied the reality of judgement, "you will not surely die", and has continued to do so ever since. He also denied the very goodness of God, suggesting that the prohibition of eating from the tree of the knowledge of good and evil had been given to keep men and women from real fulfilment and happiness: ". . . for God knows that when you eat of it your eyes will be opened and you will be like God" (Gen. 3:5). It is critical to notice here the relationship between the beliefs or doctrines people hold, and the lives they live: what men and women believe determines how they act. If the notion of judgement is eliminated from their worldview then that will necessarily have consequences for the way they conduct their lives. Similarly, if they think that

God's commandments are harmful to their best interests, they will no doubt reject them.

Moreover, the issue is also a vital one because the understanding and acceptance of truth is crucial to salvation and perseverance in the Christian faith. For example, a central issue for the gospel in all times is the identity of Christ: it is perhaps *the* fundamental theological issue. The great question that Jesus himself asked his disciples concerned his identity, and the same question echoes down through history: "who do you say I am" (Matt. 16:15). However, just a generation or two after Jesus asked that question, John warned of those who were introducing error on this very point by apparently denying the reality of the incarnation. These were people who denied that "Jesus Christ has come in the flesh" (1 John 4:1-3). Again, Paul's argument in 1 Corinthians 15 indicates that there were others who denied the resurrection, which is also central to the gospel.

In both cases the false teachers may well have been metaphysical dualists influenced by the Greek worldview, which tended to regard the material world as evil and that which is spirit as good, and therefore saw the human body as a prison of the soul. Accordingly, the notion of a true incarnation was impossible, for God could scarcely be united with human flesh if it was by nature evil, notwithstanding

John's clear declaration – "and the Word became flesh" (John 1:14). The idea of the resurrection of the body made little sense either, as it meant re- incarceration in a prison from which the deceased person had been freed. Such beliefs thus undermined the doctrines of incarnation, resurrection, and ultimately the biblical doctrine of creation. For similar reasons, some supposedly Christian teachers were forbidding marriage and the consumption of certain foods, and Paul responded by insisting on the goodness of all that God had made in creation (1 Tim. 4:1-4). It is once again especially important to recognize the way in which beliefs embedded within culture – the beliefs of worldview – may lead those who hold them to reject or distort biblical truth.

The issue arises in every generation, but in different areas of truth. Today in some quarters, it is the doctrine of God's own omniscience – especially his knowledge of the future – that is being questioned, or the utter trustworthiness of the Bible, or the substitutionary death of the Lord Jesus Christ. Again, cultural factors, in these last cases modern and Western, have led to a departure from biblical understanding.

In the African context, too, there is a continuing struggle to differentiate between beliefs that originate in culture and those that are rooted in God's word – and to ensure that the former are placed under the judgement of the latter. In the context of this present study, traditional African belief in the reality of an invisible world of spirits somewhat echoes the biblical teaching that also affirms the existence of angels, spirits, demons and so on. However, the notion – quite widespread in Africa – that all human suffering may be caused by witches, ancestors or spirits emphatically does *not* have biblical support. What it actually does is to *increase* human misery – which is exactly Satan's intention. When suffering is explained largely in terms of the activity of sorcerers, every incident of illness, every accident and adversity leads to mutual suspicion and hostility as people set out to determine who is responsible. Witch-hunts and often violent revenge follow, the whole process contributing to the destruction of community, as well as untold and unjust suffering for individuals and families. In 2001 around the town of Aru in northeast Congo, possibly between 2000 and 4000 people were "executed on suspicion of witchcraft, in a two-week killing spree."[3] The witch-hunt was provoked by the deaths of large numbers of children, which was then blamed on witches – the "night dancers". In fact, most of the infant mortality was caused by malnutrition due to the war going on at the time in that region. Satan penetrates the cultures of human societies with false values and misguided worldviews, and Christians face conflict in this whole area if their minds are to be renewed according to truth.

Throughout the history of the church there have always been those who deny fundamental truth and so there is a need for constant vigilance. This implies the necessity of a solid understanding of the truth that God has revealed, and an ability to evaluate every idea and belief in the light of it. Accordingly, Paul told Timothy to watch his life and teaching (1 Tim. 4:16), and in a similar way warned the Ephesian elders about those who would later come among them with false ideas and cause havoc among God's people:

---

[3] A. Blomfield, "Massacre by the Jungle Witch-Hunters", in the *Daily Telegraph*, 28th July 2001.

> I know that after I leave, savage wolves will come in
> among you and will not spare the flock. Even from your
> own number men will arise and distort the truth in
> order to draw away disciples after them. So be on your
> guard! (Acts 20:30-31).

The battlefront changes as Satan exploits the spirit of a
particular period or culture and fashions his attack on truth
accordingly. It is vital to know where the battle is in one's own
place and generation, and to contend for truth with courage,
especially at the point of attack (Jude 1:3). Martin Luther had
strong words to say on the issue:

> If I profess with the loudest voice and clearest
> exposition every portion of the truth of God except that
> little point which the world and the devil are at that
> moment attacking, I am not *confessing* Christ, however
> boldly I may be *professing* him. Where the battle rages,
> there the loyalty of the soldier is proved, and to be
> steady on all the battlefield besides is mere flight and
> disgrace if he flinches at that point.[4]

It should also be noted that Satan uses doctrinal disputes
over *minor* issues to ravage the church and its mission.
Sometimes we need to contend for the truth and that will
cause division which, while sad, may be necessary. Martin
Luther and others like him were driven out of the church of
Rome – they did not leave of their own accord – because they

---

[4]M. Luther, Church Postil (Minneapolis: Lutheran in All Lands Co, 1903),
quoted by D. J. Hall, "The Diversity of Christian Witnessing in the Tension
between Subjection to the Word and the Relation to the Context" in P.
Manns & H. Meyer (eds.) *Luther's Ecumenical Significance and Interconfessional
Consultation* (Philadelphia: Fortress, 1984), 257.

stood for gospel truth. However, Christians also sometimes disagree over relatively trivial issues that are not crucial to the gospel or to Christian living, such as the precise chronology surrounding Christ's return, or whether to use a single big cup or lots of little cups at the communion service. The result is unnecessary division and the marring of the testimony of the church as new congregations and denominations are set up for the feeblest of reasons, or as Christians hop around from one church to another searching for one that exactly conforms to their wishes. Paul also warns against idle speculation which promotes controversy rather than the building up of God's people in truth (1 Tim. 1:4-5; 2 Tim. 2:23), a warning which brings us to the next point.

Division

Division is fatally weakening in warfare. One of the great problems of military alliances between different nations is that of ensuring that they have and maintain common purpose and action. Similarly, in the spiritual field, Satan attacks by promoting division or schism, which is sin. The unity of the people of God must always be of immense concern to Christians. From the garden of Eden on to the present, sin has divided humanity into warring camps based on ethnicity, gender, social class, economic status, intellectual attainment and so on. The fallen world is a world of hatred, violence and war at every level. However, the purpose of the work of Christ was not only to reconcile men and women to God – although that is indeed its primary and most profound intent – but also to reconcile them to one another in the one family of the people of God. It is the very unity of

God's people which should constitute the proof that they truly are disciples of Christ – because of the love that they show for one another (John 13:35). A community of mutual love, acceptance, forbearance and forgiveness is so contrary to the nature of human relationships in the world that it provides the ultimate witness to the gospel. The world may not be able to see the relationship that Christians have with God in a physical and tangible way, but they can certainly see their relationships with one another, and it is there if anywhere that they either show the fruit of the gospel or else deny it at its most fundamental level. The sad reality is that too often life and relationships within the church are simply a mirror image of what goes on outside it, and the *word* of the gospel is undermined by the failure of believers to live it out. It is no coincidence that in beginning the section of Ephesians in which he turns to exhortation, Paul starts with the need for unity, and it is immediately clear that it does not happen without effort:

> Be completely humble and gentle; be patient, bearing with one another in love. Make every effort to keep the unity of the Spirit through the bond of peace (Eph. 4:2-3).

It is maintained through humility, patience, and tolerance of the failings and foibles of others.

Conflict occurs among the people of God over many things, including the minor doctrinal issues that we have just mentioned. There are also personality conflicts. Paul seems to have had this in mind when he exhorted Euodia and Syntyche to be reconciled with one another, and urged another Christian brother to help them sort out their differences (Phil.

4:2-3). In mission, conflict may arise over questions of strategy and practice. Paul and Barnabas divided over whether to take John Mark with them on a second journey, with the result that they could no longer work together (Acts 15:36-41). In churches, serious divisions sometimes arise over similar questions of policy which do not engage fundamental issues of truth, and on which Christians should be able to disagree harmoniously and still work and worship together. Too often people simply want their own way, and break away from others when they cannot have it regardless of the implications of their actions for the gospel and the glory of God.

There is also the threat of ethnic conflict among believers. This endangered the unity of the Jerusalem church when there was a dispute over the distribution of food to Christian widows, with accusations that one ethnic group, the Hebraic Jews, was being favoured over the other, the Grecian Jews (Acts 6:1-7). The apostles recognized the gravity of the threat to church unity and stepped in quickly to resolve the issue. It is especially important to notice that they did not deal with the problem by dividing the church into ethnic congregations. This is the approach sometimes advocated and adopted today: it solves the issue in a pragmatic way by keeping possible enemies apart. However, from a gospel perspective it is highly questionable – even heretical: it effectively contradicts the fact that the gospel unites believers across ethnic barriers, and indeed across every possible human barrier (Gal. 3:28; Col. 3:11). In doing so, it denies its power and undermines the potent testimony that real Christian unity offers to a warring world. Similarly, the Judaising controversy over whether Gentile believers needed to be circumcised or not was fundamentally doctrinal in tone, but also had clear ethnic implications and threatened to halt the advance of the gospel in its tracks. The council of Jerusalem sought to resolve the issue in such a way that gentile and Jewish believers could worship together in the same churches and in their own homes (Acts 15). Traces of the dispute continue throughout the New Testament.

There are far too often conflicts over power, when people fight one another to have the highest positions and the church is divided in consequence. On at least three occasions the twelve disciples of Jesus disputed among themselves the right to the supreme position, even when Jesus was still physically with them – and indeed even at the last supper as Jesus spoke of his imminent death (Mark 9:33-37; 10:35-45; Luke 22:24-30). Much later the apostle John warned about a certain Diotrephes who evidently wanted the top place, and whose pursuit of power caused division: "Diotrephes, who loves to be first, will have nothing to do with us" (3 John 9). Human lust for power is insatiable, and is rooted in the first sin – the desire to be like God. Satan has fed it from the beginning in order to cause division and violence, thereby bringing about untold human suffering – even within the church. Churches are ravaged and destroyed by the craving for power.

And finally, once again, the logic of witchcraft belief is one very significant means by which Satan stirs division within society, and all too often within the church as well. The evil of witchcraft is not only the possibility of its actual practice, but even more the hatred and violence engendered by the belief itself. Traditional witchcraft belief produces an underlying atmosphere of fear and suspicion, and one which quickly

surfaces when there is a misfortune or some unusual event.
The feeling that neighbours, kin, fellow church members,
may have killed members of one's own family inevitably
causes hatred and exacerbates the ordinary tensions of human
relationships, leading eventually to cruelty and even death.[5]
The tendency of witchcraft belief is to tear society – and
churches – apart. It is a tragedy when Christians, who should
be peacemakers, subscribe to a system of thought that is so
totally destructive.

It is most significant that in the New Testament three
particular issues are singled out for the censure of church
discipline: immorality (1 Cor. 5:1-5), doctrinal error (1 Tim.
1:18-20), and division (Titus 3:10-11) – the three issues we
have just been dealing with.

Hostility and fear

Fear is one of Satan's choice battlefields and he uses that
fear to hinder the progress of the gospel. At its heart, fear
means doubting God and his ability to protect and guide,
and in consequence Satan is able to cripple believers in what
they should be doing. Fear initially paralysed the disciples of
Jesus after his crucifixion (John 20:19), and it seems quite
likely that it caused the return of John Mark from Paul and
Barnabas's first missionary journey, although the exact reason
is not altogether clear (Acts 13:13). Timothy may have been
a naturally timid individual, great servant of God though he
was, and Paul encouraged him to recognize the power of
the Spirit who indwelt him (2 Tim. 1:7-8). In the context

---

[5]See also M. Hunter, *Reaction to Conquest* (London: Oxford University Press,
1936), 318-9.

of his well-known passage on spiritual warfare, Paul himself asked for prayer for boldness; it is significant that the word "fearlessly" is used twice, which indicates the apostle's own awareness of the way in which fear could lead to paralysis (Eph. 6:19-20). Elsewhere, he acknowledges how his initial proclamation in Corinth took place "in weakness and fear, and with much trembling" (1 Cor. 2:3). Similarly, in the earliest days of the church, following the first threats against them, the disciples gathered together and prayed, not for the removal of the threats but for renewed boldness to preach the gospel (Acts 4:29). It is significant that when Jesus warned the disciples of coming opposition, he exhorted them to 'take heart'; "But take heart! I have overcome the world" (John 16:33). He well understood the human heart, and the danger that his disciples would lose courage as they faced opposition from the world. Discouragement can also take other forms. Satan is the accuser, and one aspect of his accusation is to give believers a sense of failure and worthlessness, and so discourage them in their task. The answer is to understand that all our failure and sin are already dealt with at the cross: we have overcome Satan already – "by the blood of the Lamb" (Rev. 12:11).

Fear is the natural response to the threat of violence. Physical aggression was a feature of Satanic and worldly opposition to the gospel and the people of God in the New Testament, and this has continued to be true throughout the history of the church. In the case of the violence suffered by the Lord Jesus Christ himself, it was Satan who inspired Judas in the act of betrayal that led to the crucifixion (John 13:2, 27). Jesus warned his disciples that in the world they too would have trouble (John 16:33), that following him meant taking up a cross (Mark 8:34- 38), and that if the world had persecuted him then it would persecute them too (John 15:20). In Revelation, Satan inspired the persecution of the "children of the woman" – that is, the church (Rev. 12:13-13:18). Paul especially emphasized the place of suffering in Christian life and ministry, and he reminded other believers – including the Philippians – that it was an integral part of faithful discipleship,

> For it has been granted to you on behalf of Christ not only to believe on him, but also to suffer for him, since you are going through the same struggle you saw I had, and now hear that I still have (Phil. 1:29-30; see also Acts 14:22).

The narrative of Acts demonstrates that throughout his missionary travels Paul experienced unremitting opposition including frequent physical attack, and in the letters to the Corinthians he referred repeatedly to the trials he endured – which he regarded not as exceptional occurrences, but rather as the proof of his faithfulness in the service of Christ:

> Are they servants of Christ? . . . I am more. I have worked much harder, been in prison more frequently, been flogged more severely, and been exposed to death again and again (2 Cor. 11:23).

Indeed, he points out that it is precisely *through* the suffering of his servants that the gospel of Christ advances in the world. It is human weakness, as manifested most clearly at the cross of Christ, that is the context in which the power of God is demonstrated:

> For we who are alive are always being given over to death for Jesus' sake, so that his life may be revealed

in our mortal body. So then, death is at work in us, but
life is at work in you (2 Cor. 4:11-12).

Opposition comes from many sources. Both Jesus and Paul
suffered opposition and persecution from the Jewish religious
establishment of their day. In Ephesus, Paul encountered
hostility from defenders of the pagan worship of Diana,
although commercial interests threatened by the gospel
were also profoundly implicated (Acts 19:23-4). Throughout
history the church has faced persecution from antagonistic
religious interests of whatever sort. Moreover, although it is
the means ordained in God's providence for the maintenance
of justice (Rom. 13:1-7), the state has in certain times and
places become an instrument of satanic despotism, often
allying itself with religious opposition to the gospel. The
author of Revelation used symbolic terms to describe just such
a process taking place in the late first-century Roman empire
of Domitian. The dragon, Satan, summoned the beast out of
the deep reservoir of evil to make war on the people of God:

> And the dragon stood on the shore of the sea. And I
> saw a beast coming out of the sea . . . He was given
> power to make war against the saints and to conquer
> them (Rev. 12:1, 7).

What is once more striking, however, is the author's
conviction that even this happened subject to God's own
sovereign rule. In the phrase, "he was given power", he uses
the passive form of the verb – sometimes referred to in such
contexts as a 'divine passive' – to indicate that even as the
beast attacked God's people, it was, in fact, God himself who
had given it the power to do so. God was fulfilling his own far
greater purposes through its wickedness.

Moreover, political and social disorder and corruption – the world's conflicts and greed – may well hinder the progress of the gospel. After his arrest, Paul was unjustly kept in custody by the Roman governor, Felix, who was waiting for him to come up with a bribe for his release (Acts 24:26). It is significant that Paul was aware of what was going on in Felix's mind, but did not offer money for his own release, nor ask his friends to do so, even though it meant waiting in prison for two years when he might have been continuing with his ministry outside.

Those who practise magic and sorcery may also oppose believers and the gospel under the inspiration of Satan. One clear example is that of Elymas, whom Paul identified as "a child of the devil" when he opposed Paul's preaching and tried to turn the Roman proconsul of Cyprus away from the faith (Acts 13:10). Simon Magus, the magician of Samaria, attempted to corrupt the apostles with money when they went to Samaria, in an effort to add the Holy Spirit to his own occult powers (Acts 8:18-19). Moreover, while Satan may inflict physical harm on believers through human intermediaries, it is also possible for him to injure them directly. We have already noticed that Paul identified the "thorn in the flesh" (probably a physical affliction) which he suffered with "a messenger from Satan" (2 Cor. 12:7). His readers would almost certainly have identified the "messenger from Satan" as a demon; thus he is saying that he suffered from some physical affliction whose immediate source was demonic. Similarly, in the Old Testament God permitted Satan himself to afflict Job and his family, resulting in the loss of his children, his riches and his health (Job 1-2).

It is very important, however, to recognize once again that in both cases suffering took place in the context of God's sovereignty. Satan could do nothing against Job without divine permission, nor could he go beyond the limits that God set. This is very clear in the opening chapters of the book. Similarly, the language Paul uses implies that God was the ultimate cause of his suffering. Therefore, like the author of Revelation, he too uses the passive form of the verb, "there was given me a thorn in my flesh, a messenger of Satan, to torment me" (2 Cor. 12:7), which implies that God was behind the activity of the satanic messenger. Further, the text says that through the trial God was working out his good purpose, that of preserving Paul from conceit and so ensuring that he would continue to be useful as a servant of the gospel—"for when I am weak, then I am strong" (2 Cor. 12:10). This means that believers are delivered from the futile arbitrariness of demonic hostility and, as with Paul's "thorn", their sufferings take on positive meaning and value. In brief, God uses them for good (Rom. 5:3; 8:28-39; James 1:2-4; 1 Pet. 1:6-7). Moreover, through Christ they have access to divine resources which enable them both to resist and to endure attacks made upon them (2 Cor. 12:8-10; Rev. 2:10). Satan may inflict pain on believers but never outside of God's sovereign purpose; he is always and only a creature, and is subject, as all creatures are, to God's rule over his creation.

In this context, one particular question is whether demons can possess Christians. The traditional answer has probably been to deny such a possibility, but there is a good deal of disagreement. However, there are solid grounds for retaining the traditional approach. From a theological perspective, the

New Testament identifies Christians as temples of the Holy Spirit (1 Cor. 6:19), and it must be problematic to suppose that a Christian who is indwelt by God's Spirit could at the same time be 'possessed' by a demon. Is it conceivable that the Holy Spirit and an unclean spirit might 'inhabit' the same person at the same time? Second, by definition a Christian is somebody who has been freed from bondage to Satan. Demonic possession can be seen, however, as the most extreme expression of Satan's tyranny over human beings. Again, it does not seem plausible that an individual might, on the one hand, be freed from Satan's tyranny and, on the other hand, remain a victim of one of its most extreme forms.

Third, the Bible itself offers little or no support for the idea that Christians can be possessed. In their numerous epistles the New Testament writers deal with a wide range of pastoral issues, but nowhere do they respond to difficulties in the Christian life by suggesting that a demon may be the cause of them, and that expulsion would accordingly be the answer. Insofar as believers experienced problems in their lives, the answer seems to have been repentance, obedience, the filling of the Holy Spirit, perseverance and faithfulness, and so on – but nowhere the expulsion of demons.

Fourth, there is the issue of experience. Some writers have claimed that *in practice* – in experience – liberation from demons has helped some Christians to move to a higher level of Christian life and service. However, such an approach in turn raises rather larger issues, and especially whether questions of Christian faith and practice are to be determined by the word of God or by human experience. Moreover, it is clear that the *meaning* of experience may be ambiguous, and that experiences can often be interpreted in more than one way. Thus, on this particular issue, there are cases of believers who have experienced sufferings which might well have been identified as possession, but which have, in fact, been resolved by approaches quite other than the expulsion of invading demons. On the other hand, there are those who have gone through a procedure which apparently delivered them from demonic possession, only for the effects of the deliverance to have lasted but a brief period before the symptoms reappeared. It is possible to question whether some 'exorcisms' may in fact be hypnotic episodes which persuade victims that they have been delivered, and in that sense effect a cure. The issue is clearly not simple.[6]

Finally, there is the critical danger of minimising sin. Human depravity can ruin lives, including Christian lives. It is possible to attribute to demons what in fact should be attributed to sin, and to pursue the expulsion of demons when it is repentance that is actually called for. Nowhere does the Bible explain human sin in terms of demonic possession: the biblical solution to sin is repentance and not the expulsion of a demon of jealousy or hatred or whatever. Similarly, if somebody is ill, the expulsion of demons will not normally be part of the treatment, but prayer and confession will be (James 5:14-16).

Nevertheless, the possibility that believers may be *troubled* by demonic and occult activity – even with serious effects – should not be discounted. This would certainly fall short of actually being *demonised* or *possessed* in the sense intended

---

[6]For a much fuller discussion of this issue see D. Powlison, *Power Encounters: Reclaiming Spiritual Warfare* (Grand Rapids: Baker, 1995).

by the synoptic gospel writers. However, especially in a missionary context, as the gospel is being brought for the first time among people long held captive by Satan, he may use various methods to discourage and incapacitate both those who bring good news and those who respond to it. Missionaries have spoken of satanic attack in such situations, including attacks on their children, on their health (both physical and emotional), an awareness of evil presences and phenomena in their homes, and so on. The brief narrative at the beginning of chapter 4, recounting the serious satanic oppression that James Fraser experienced in 1913-1914 as he sought to bring the gospel to the Lisu people, is a striking example of this. And of course, the same may also be true in other situations. Christians facing extreme forms of disturbance in their lives need to be treated with pastoral care and sensitivity, and surrounded by prayer, but one should be rather wary about jumping to the conclusion that they are actually possessed by demons. One should equally be wary of the danger of interpreting frightening or distressing experiences in terms of some sort of demonic manifestation, when they may perhaps be understood in a more mundane fashion. There is a need for balance in this whole area, and especially as demonic interpretations of experience risk becoming fashionable. Any authentically Christian answer *must* be based on a careful and honest reading of Scripture.

In every situation of opposition and persecution, Satan's ultimate purpose is to discourage believers and, if possible, bring about apostasy from the faith. His aim is not merely to harm them physically, but spiritually: it is eternal death, and not physical death, that he really wants to bring about.

In a biblical perspective, there is something infinitely worse than physical pain and suffering, and that is apostasy. This has dire, eternal consequences far beyond any immediate physical anguish that may result from illness or persecution. Jesus made this point very clearly when he spoke of the awfulness of divine judgement:

> I tell you, my friends, do not be afraid of those who kill the body and after that can do no more. But I will show you whom you should fear: Fear him who, after the killing of the body, has power to throw you into hell. Yes, I tell you, fear him (Luke 12:4- 5).

Consequently, in the face of persecution and bodily or emotional pain, Satan is defeated by those who remain faithful. They overcome him, because "they did not love their lives so much as to shrink from death" (Rev. 12:11).

Conclusion

The Bible bears consistent witness to the warfare with which God's people have to contend. It is multifaceted, and their great enemy seeks to exploit their weaknesses to cause harm, even eternal harm. For Satan's goal in this is not so much to inflict physical pain or temporary discomfort on them, but lasting spiritual damage. It is, moreover, at this point that there is a striking contrast with notions of spirit attack found in traditional African religion. The harm that spirits and sorcerers inflict there is primarily physical and material: they bring illness, accident, barrenness and drought, the loss of crops and livestock, or failure in some enterprise – including, in the modern world, sport, romance, or business. The Bible recognizes that the devil does attack in these ways: the book of Job speaks of a man who lost children, possessions and health from satanic attack. However, Satan's goal even in that situation was not so much the physical losses that Job incurred, grievous as they were; his purpose was rather to provoke a reaction of apostasy – cursing God – through the material loss and bodily pain. In biblical terms, the greatest evil is not physical pain and suffering, but separation from the Creator.

While African tradition recognizes the existence of a spiritual domain, and the fact that it can be harmful to human beings – although at this point there is a good deal of ambiguity – it does not recognize the true nature or depth of the evil that dark and hostile spirits seek to bring upon men and women. While one must not minimise the real grief and pain that physical loss may entail, the African perception of the harm that spirits cause is nevertheless *relatively* very superficial when compared with what the Bible has to say about them.

Its conception of salvation is also, therefore, partial and inadequate, being at best the temporary repulse of physical ills. The real threat that Satan poses is his ambition to separate human beings from God forever, and so to ensure their eternal death. Real victory over him does not, therefore, consist in the successful protection of material interests and physical health from his attacks, but in resisting his temptations in every area of life, and remaining faithful – even to the point of death. "Be faithful, even to the point of death, and I will give you the crown of life" (Rev. 2:10).

Questions for further reflection

1. Why do redeemed men and women still struggle with temptation?

2. Identify the sins that are especially characteristic of your culture.

3. Where are the world and the devil especially attacking Christian truth in your context today?

4. Are there ever circumstances in which it is appropriate for Christians to separate from a church?

5. Why do we fear?

6. Can a Christian be 'possessed' by a demon?

7. What should Christians do about witches and belief in witchcraft?

CHAPTER 6

THE WEAPONS OF OUR WARFARE

Early in the morning of April 17, 1937, Italian army trucks came to take us and our few belongings to Addis Ababa. There were twenty-six of us going – nineteen missionaries and seven children. The trucks were part of an army convoy, and the officers insisted we leave promptly. But it was most difficult to break away – to make the last embrace, the last handshake. …

When the missionaries came in 1928 there was not a single Wallamo believer, nothing of the Bible in their language, no knowledge of Jesus and the new life that comes through believing in Him. Now, after just nine years, there was a small church – part of the invisible body of Christ. A group of forty-eight baptized believers were all living witnesses of the tremendous change the gospel had made in Wallamo life.

As we turned the last corner around the mountain and saw in the distance the wave of their hands in farewell, we wondered what would happen to the little flickering flame of Gospel light that had been lit in the midst of so much darkness. Would these young Christians, with no more of the Word of God in their own language than the Gospel of Mark and a few small booklets of selected Scripture portions to guide and teach them, be able to stand under the persecution that would inevitably come?

...

[Five years later] *"When you missionaries left, it was difficult to find a Christian in Wallamo country. Now it is difficult to find a man who is not a Christian."* . . *Such a sweeping statement, how could it be true? . . Was it really possible that the Gospel light had not been snuffed out but was blazing more strongly than ever?*

Questioning the Wallamo visitor only magnified the original statement to greater proportions. Yes, great numbers of Wallamo people had turned to the Lord. The village life – in fact the entire tribal life of the southern country had been transformed. There were now perhaps 100 separate churches, and probably 10,000 believers in Wallamo. ...

The year was 1942. Ethiopia was beginning to recover from the shock of war, but as yet no missionaries had been allowed to return.

Thousands had believed the message in spite of persecution. All thought of the missionaries as those "who had brought us God's matter" – but none of them, even those who had known the missionaries, ever expected to see missionaries again. "Our only hope, we thought, was to meet you in God's country," they said. ...

The first three months on their own were a time of testing and self- examination with a great deal of prayer.

Then the fire came. Or, as Ato Ginja described it, "As thirsty cattle turn toward the tasty water, so the people began to turn to God. They left their Satan worship and pagan practices."

The tiny churches began sending out preachers, two by two, baptizing those who had believed for some time. Soon even the unbelievers were keen to hear God's Word. As many hundreds

*turned to God, branch churches were established. By the second
year it was necessary to build church buildings and choose local
elders.* [1]

God does not leave his people defenceless as they face spiritual
warfare; neither does he expect that they will respond to the
conflict with passivity. The Bible gives abundant direction
about the conduct of the fight, as well as warnings about
inappropriate warfare – warnings to which the church and
individual believers have not always paid sufficient attention.

How then should Christians fight as they face the world,
the flesh and the devil? There are numerous issues to bear in
mind.

Spiritual weapons

First of all, the church and individual believers must never
respond to attack by using the methods and weapons of the
world – and indeed those of Satan himself. Paul's words to
the Corinthians on this subject are vitally important: "though
we live in the world, we do not wage war as the world does.
The weapons we fight with are not the weapons of the world"
(2 Cor. 10:3-4). When Peter drew his sword in the garden
of Gethsemane to defend Jesus from arrest, he resorted to
human weapons in a conflict where they were totally useless.
He failed to appreciate the nature of the battle which was
about to take place – a battle which would be won not by steel
but by the death of the Saviour. A crucial factor in all such
cases is that of recognising the 'depth' of the spiritual conflict:

---

[1] R. J. Davis, *Fire on the Mountains* (SIM, 1980), passim 100-114. Reproduced
by permission of SIM International, Fort Mill, South Carolina, U.S.A.

Christians sometimes resort to the use of human weapons because they can see only human enemies and fail to identify the powers that stand behind them. However, the ultimate adversary they have to contend with is not other human beings, nor hostile governments or adverse circumstances, but Satan himself.

Jesus' final words at Gethsemane, as his 'human' foes closed in to arrest him, indicate his awareness of the much deeper dynamic that lay at the heart of the more obvious hostility of those who came to seize him:

> Am I leading a rebellion, that you have come with swords and clubs? Every day I was with you in the temple courts, and you did not lay a hand on me. But this is your hour—when darkness reigns (Luke 22:52-53).

Paul recognized the same thing in the context of his own ministry:

> . . . for our struggle is not against flesh and blood, but against the rulers, against the authorities, against the powers of this dark world and against the spiritual forces of evil in the heavenly realms (Eph. 6:12).

It is significant that he wrote those words when he was imprisoned as a result of the hostility of Jewish leaders and the cowardly complicity of Roman authorities, and so might well have been tempted to focus on the human dimension of his captivity.

It is easy to lash out – overtly or subtly, verbally or physically – against those who hurt or hinder us in our Christian lives and ministries, while failing to realize that ultimately they are not the real enemy at all. What is needed is a spiritual perception and wisdom that are biblical and balanced. Christians must be able to see beyond the obvious, visible difficulties to the underlying spiritual realities that confront them. The New Testament warns more than once about Satan's subtlety and wiles (2 Cor. 2:11; Eph. 6:11). It is easy to forget about them, to fall into his snares and make matters worse by attacking, even perhaps physically attacking, human beings, due to a failure to recognize the spiritual element in the struggle. It is equally possible of course – and this is where balance is critical – to attribute every failure on our own part or in our ministries to the devil, and fail to take responsibility for them ourselves.

Through the centuries, Peter's error has been constantly repeated whenever the church has resorted to the use of violence to achieve its goals. In eighth-century Europe, the Frankish emperor Charlemagne conquered the Saxon people – and then 'converted' them on pain of death, forcing them to be baptised as Christians. In the sixteenth century, European powers subdued and 'converted' ancient South American kingdoms, armed with the faith in the one hand and the sword in the other. Both Catholics and Protestants have used state power to impose church discipline against 'heretics', using military conquest, physical torture and even the death penalty. Perhaps most notorious of all was the crusaders' attempt to recover Palestine from the Muslims which, far from serving the cause of the gospel, effectively denied it. The very use of the word, *crusade*, originating as it does from the Latin *crux* (*cross*), draws attention to the Christian warriors' dire misunderstanding of Christian warfare and the meaning of the cross in Christian witness. There was a fatal contradiction at the very heart of their project; it was a travesty of Christian mission, and the resulting centuries of bitterness with all the implications for evangelism among Muslims, are proof enough of the disastrous effects of waging war as the world does.

Nor should the use of carnal weapons be regarded as an error limited to Christians living in more unenlightened periods of history. The use of manipulative psychological techniques in evangelism may not involve physical violence, but certainly implies violence of another kind. Christians are not exempt from the temptation to engage in political manoeuvring, or to use gossip, half-truth and whispering campaigns to advance the interests of their particular ecclesiastical parties, or to further ethnic and family interests within churches and Christian organisations.

Moreover, some churches use decidedly unspiritual weapons in their response to human fears of the witch. Among them there are church leaders who claim to be able to deliver witch suspects from the spirits which allegedly empower them, often in exchange for monetary payment. The practice certainly draws in new members, but it looks much like a corrupt exploitation of the witchcraft phobias of the surrounding society in order to increase church numbers and to make financial gain. Then there are churches which use brutal methods to extract confessions from witch suspects, even from children accused of being witches:

> The healing ceremonies took place in the revivalist churches. One pastor burned my body with candles. A prophet mama covered my body with a red cloth. In yet another church, they poured the sap from a tree

into my eyes. It stung terribly. The healer said that the witchcraft had gone. My eyes hurt so badly.[2]

In 1692, in Salem Village, a small settlement in Massachusetts, North America, there was an outbreak of paranoia against witches, and accusations led to the execution of 20 people. Most of those involved in the witch-hunt were believers, but as time went on they came to recognise the disastrous mistake that they had made in engaging in a tragically misconceived form of spiritual warfare, and they publicly confessed their error:

> . . . we justly fear that we were sadly deluded and mistaken . . . we also pray that we may be considered candidly, and aright by the living Sufferers, as being then under the power of a strong and general Delusion . . . We do heartily ask forgiveness of you all . . .[3]

Believers need to think through what is really taking place when a person falls ill, and suspicion, accusation, and perhaps violent attack on witch suspects follow. Satan seeks to gain footholds in the church of Christ in order to divide and destroy, and the things we have been discussing – accusation, the violent extraction of confessions, and so on – give him ample opportunity. There is no biblical basis for seeing accusations of witchcraft as a weapon of Christian spiritual warfare. The only accusation that can have any validity at all is where a person has been clearly, identifiably and unmistakably seen engaging in known occult rites by

---

[2]Quoted by Cimpric, *Children Accused of Witchcraft*, 35.

[3]G. Harrison, 'Witchcraft in Salem' in *Fulfilling the Great Commission* (London: The Westminster Conference, 1992), 128.

more than one trustworthy witness. Even that would not necessarily mean that the accused had actually harmed somebody. Insubstantial accusations – accusations based on such things as dreams, the supposed words of demons, 'revelation' through a 'prophet' or 'healer' – should be simply rejected. In such cases what is taking place is the syncretistic introduction of traditional practices of divination or witch-finding into a superficially Christian framework. As a result, the Christian faith is gradually transformed into a new form of traditional magic.

Similarly, a confession of witchcraft activity should only be accepted where the person involved is of totally sound mind, and confesses entirely voluntarily and under no form of duress whatsoever, including psychological and emotional pressure as well as physical torture. Confession made by a person suffering from some form of depression or other mental instability is totally inadmissible. Equally, any sort of witchcraft confession by a child should be treated with immense caution. Children are vulnerable, suggestible, and easily manipulated by psychological pressure, not to mention physical abuse. "A child who is repeatedly told that he or she is a witch may eventually believe and even act upon it."[4]

Spiritual warfare is characterized above all by truth and righteousness (Eph. 6:14) as we shall see, and the principles which guided Paul's practice need to be constantly reaffirmed in every place and generation: "we have renounced secret and shameful ways; we do not use deception, nor do we distort the word of God" (2 Cor. 4:2).

---

[4]E. Van Der Meer, 'The Problem of Witchcraft in Malawi' in *EMQ 47.1* (January 2011).

Intelligence

Given that Satan – the "liar and the father of lies" (John 8:44) – is the one with whom Christians must contend, their own grasp of truth necessarily occupies a central place in their spiritual warfare. As we have seen, Satan attacks through the denial or distortion of truth to bring about failure and defeat. He knows well that human lives and behaviour are largely shaped by what goes on in human minds – by the convictions, attitudes and values that all men and women have. His primeval temptation seduced Eve through deception and lies, the aim of which was to undermine her grasp on truth – denying the reality of judgement, impugning the goodness of God, and suggesting that the violation of God's commandment was the route to human fulfilment. The same pattern of temptation has continued ever since the fall in Eden, and he blinds human minds to prevent people from perceiving truth (2 Cor. 4:4).

Paul refers to a battle for the mind which is fundamental to Christian life and ministry:

> We demolish arguments and every pretension that sets itself up against the knowledge of God, and we take captive every thought to make it obedient to Christ (2 Cor. 10:5).

In the first place, this battle concerns *worldview*. Some belief system or other will always control human intelligence and behaviour: minds are formed and actions consequently determined by an internal map of reality which is being shaped from the earliest years of life through surrounding culture and all its influences – parents, peers, the media and so on. Behind these influences there is the hidden presence of the 'world' in rebellion against its Creator, and of the 'prince' of that world, keeping it in darkness and manipulating it to achieve his own ends.

For example, the pagan worldview of Paul's day was one in which adultery, fornication, and even homosexuality were scarcely regarded as evils. The Greek society of the earliest Christian churches was, therefore, largely oblivious to the problem of sexual sin – as Western society has become once again. Thus, in many of his letters Paul vigorously challenges the unconscious assumptions of his newly converted readers concerning the acceptability or irrelevance of sexual sin: "do you now know that he who unites himself with a prostitute is one with her in body?" (1 Cor. 6:16). Similarly, his very negative remarks about Cretans in his letter to Titus ("Cretans are always liars, evil brutes, lazy gluttons") reflect the fact that whole cultures may become corrupt in one particular area or another, with immense consequences for the life of the community as a whole (Titus 1:12-13).

The problem is aggravated in that the beliefs and assumptions drawn from culture are invariably held unconsciously – without thinking, such that people may be largely insensible to elements of corruption within the society they belong to. Believers need, therefore, to bring worldview beliefs deliberately into their own consciousness and submit them to the judgement of the word of Christ. They must be alert to the thinking and values of their cultures and to the way in which they exercise control over their lives. If not they will remain passively and involuntarily subject to them. Accordingly, if Satan battles to plant and nourish lies in the thinking of Christians through whatever means, their response

– the fundamental weapon of their warfare – must be so to feed and reflect on the word of God and its implications, that their minds, and in turn their lives, are reshaped by it. It is for this reason that, as Paul moves from the doctrinal section of Romans to its practical application, he speaks of the necessity for minds to be renewed in order that lives should no longer be shaped by the world's thinking: "do not conform any longer to the pattern of this world, but be transformed by the renewing of your mind" (Rom. 12:2). Minds shape lives; we are what we think. Thus, facing the hostility of Satan and of the world demands a firm grasp of the foundational tenets of Christian faith and their implications for life.

In the particular context of the present study, this means that beliefs about the invisible world of Satan and spirits and its significance for human beings must be carefully evaluated in the light of divine truth. Among other things, it is vital to understand that God is creator and absolutely sovereign over all that he has made. Satan is no more than a creature. He is, no doubt, a powerful creature with immense intelligence and range, far beyond those of human beings, but he is a creature nonetheless and does not possess the attributes of divinity, including omniscience, omnipotence, and omnipresence. He was made by God and remains always subject to God's sovereignty – unable to exceed the boundaries by which God limits his action. Of similar importance is the fact that Jesus Christ has already decisively overcome Satan, whose final destiny is therefore certain, and that, as the sovereign Lord, Jesus is now exalted far above every evil power. Moreover, because believers are *in Christ*, they are exalted with him and enjoy total security in him (Eph. 2:6), as well as being indwelt by the Holy Spirit who is a Spirit of power and love and self-control, able to sustain them in the conflict they face.

Therefore, because of who God is, and because of all that he has done in Christ, and because of the work of the Spirit in the believer's life, the Christian is an optimist when faced by Satan even though he knows that the battle may be hard. His optimism is not simply the subjective response of a naturally cheerful disposition, but it is rooted in truths that shape his mind: it derives from the renewing of the mind through the word of God. Once again, what we truly believe determines how we will act and react. Conversely, a failure to appreciate the significance of Christ's victory or the reality of God's absolute sovereignty over all that he has made, inevitably entails spiritual and moral weakness, a lack of confidence and even defeatism in the face of battle. Consequently, when confronted by tribulation, suffering and danger there will be the resort to the traditional means of defence – a consultation with the diviner, perhaps, and recourse to the protection supposedly offered by fetishes.

Closely related to this is the way in which a culture identifies the source of human pain. The universality of suffering means that questions about health, sickness and death are always and everywhere among the most important that human beings face, and responses to them are shaped by foundational worldview assumptions. As one example, Buddhism as a religion and worldview emerged from the Buddha's reflections on this very issue of human suffering. Meanwhile, the modern Western approach to pain is largely based on the naturalistic and materialistic worldview that has developed over recent centuries. As we have already noted, in traditional African understanding suffering is almost always caused *by somebody* – perhaps an ancestor, or some other malevolent spirit, or a sorcerer. Some traditional societies have tended to explain *every* ill, including death, in terms of witchcraft. The result in such cases is a state of almost perpetual anxiety or mutual suspicion for, of course, suffering is a constant of human experience; there is always some affliction to be explained, always another witch to be discovered and punished, another spirit to be identified and appeased.

At times, societies that hold strongly to such beliefs are engulfed in paranoiac witch-hunts in which large numbers of suspects may be 'purged'. After the purge, people and animals once again start falling ill, rain stops falling, barrenness occurs, there are accidents – and so the whole cycle of fear, suspicion, recrimination and violence recommences. Therefore, as a philosophy that explains suffering, witchcraft is brutally destructive: human community is undermined by endemic mistrust, and those accused of witchcraft may suffer vicious consequences for their alleged, invisible crimes. Indeed, a worldview in which witchcraft beliefs play a dominant role simply advances Satan's own essentially murderous and destructive purposes, while totally failing to deal with the problem of suffering. None of this denies the possibility of witchcraft aggression by some individuals against others; we have already noted the biblical recognition of the *possibility* of demonically empowered and harmful magic. However, an understanding of reality shaped by the biblical perspective would also see that it is human fallenness rather than the aggression of the sorcerer which is the prime source of all suffering, thereby displacing witches from the dominant role much of traditional Africa has given them – and so bringing freedom, not least from Satan's lies.

Christians must also seek to control what passes through their minds at a moral level. The human mind is always active – there is never a moment when it is simply empty, disengaged or passive, even in sleep. What passes through the mind has an effect – at every point it leaves a deposit for good or ill. It is very easy to allow one's rambling thoughts to dwell on unhelpful things: immorality, envy, hatred, bitterness, anxiety, doubt, fear, and so on. Without doubt, Satan and the fallen world around us seek to suggest such thoughts. Those thoughts then shape attitudes – and from that basis they determine words and acts and whole lives. For this reason, Paul exhorts believers to control what passes through their own minds so that they allow only what is good to find a place:

> . . . whatever is true, whatever is noble, whatever is
> right, whatever is pure, whatever is lovely, whatever is
> admirable – if anything is excellent or praiseworthy –
> think about such things (Phil. 4:8).

There needs to be an intentional and conscious vetting of the shifting currents of our minds, an awareness that even at the level of idle thought the spiritual battle is being fought, and either won or lost. Unhelpful, negative and sinful thoughts may come into our minds suddenly and apparently from nowhere, and we cannot stop them, but we can refuse to allow them to stay and instead deliberately focus our minds on "whatever is true, whatever is noble . . . " In the much quoted words of Martin Luther,

. . . you cannot prevent the birds from flying in the air over your head, but you can prevent them from building a nest in your hair. So, as St. Augustine says, we cannot prevent offenses and temptations, but by prayer and invocation of the help of God we can prevent them from overcoming us.[5]

Righteousness and truth

Paul's discussion of the *armour* of God near the end of Ephesians is well known, but the passage is sometimes detached from its context, which then obscures its meaning. The Ephesian epistle can be divided into two main sections. The first three chapters are primarily doctrinal and speak of all that God has done for his redeemed people in Christ. Then, as in other epistles, Paul goes on to discuss the implications of the truth he has been expounding for the everyday lives of his readers: "As a prisoner for the Lord, then, I urge you to live a life worthy of the calling you have received" (Eph. 4:1). This section, beginning in chapter four, continues through to chapter six where the passage on the "armour of God" – opening with the words, "for the rest" – brings the exhortation to a conclusion. Therefore, the *armour* should probably be understood in the light of that lengthy exhortation. In speaking of God's provision for them in their warfare, Paul is in fact reminding the Ephesian believers that, as they attempt to "live a life worthy of the calling" they have received, they will face the opposition of Satan and of all the

---

[5]Martin Luther, *The Lord's Prayer Explained*, in John Nicholas Lenker (translator), *Luther's Two Catechisms Explained by Himself in Six Classic Writings* (Minneapolis: The Luther Press, 1908), 305.

dark spiritual forces at his command. To be more specific – and in the light of the preceding chapters – if they seek to bear with one another in love and maintain the unity of the Spirit (4:2), to do honest work (4:28), to speak wholesome words (4:29), to maintain sexual purity (5:2-5), and to uphold God-honouring relationships (5:22-6:9), they will have to fight "against the rulers, against the authorities, against the powers of this dark world and against the spiritual forces of evil in the heavenly realms." It is precisely the purpose of these forces to undermine their testimony in all of those areas and, if it were possible, to bring them back into the slavery of sin and death.

Apart from anything else it may teach, the passage is, therefore, a vital reminder that spiritual warfare is not mostly about driving out demons from the possessed or resisting the evil magic of sorcerers, but rather that it takes place in the ordinary and everyday areas of human life. Satan's purpose is to attack Christians' family lives, their varied relationships, their sexual purity and so on. And, from the perspective of believers, the conflict is – for the most part – defensive: they are called upon to "stand" their ground as they face the assault of the powers of darkness. They do not go looking for trouble, challenging evil spirits and so on, but they need to be ready to meet trouble when it comes:

> . . . put on the full armour of God, so that when the day of evil comes, you may be able to stand your ground, and after you have done everything, to stand (Eph. 6:13).

Therefore, having urged the Ephesian believers to adopt a Christian lifestyle in every part of their lives, Paul warns them that as they try to do so, they will face a battle in which their survival will depend on their putting on "the full armour of God". The phrase itself is significant. First, Paul draws the imagery from the Old Testament where the armour is that which God himself wears. Believers deal with evil powers in the same way that God does – through righteousness, truth and the rest: "He put on righteousness as his breastplate, and the helmet of salvation on his head" (Isa. 59:17; compare to 11:4-5). Secondly, the armour is not just that which God himself uses, but he is also its source – the great armourer of his people. The description of the armour, therefore, expounds the meaning of Paul's preliminary exhortation, "be strong in the Lord and in his mighty power" (Eph. 6:10): disciples are 'strong in the Lord' as they take up the armour that he provides. Thirdly, believers are required deliberately to clothe themselves in the armour. There is nothing automatic about their protection; the fact that divine armour is available does not remove their responsibility to equip themselves with it. Finally, the first pieces of armour are identified as truth and righteousness: they are fundamentally moral attributes, which must characterize life and ministry, and we have already noted their importance in discussing the spiritual nature of the warfare that Christians face.

Truth here is probably primarily a reference to inner integrity rather than to the truth of God's word, which comes later ("the sword of the Spirit which is the word of God"). It is about the absence of hypocrisy, deviousness and sham. Its nature is reflected, for example, in Paul's remarkable testimony to Timothy's character, that he alone of all his associates truly pursued the interests of Christ Jesus (Phil. 2:20-22); the nature of Timothy's life and ministry showed that there was a profound sincerity and reality at the heart of his Christian profession. Success in the face of Satan's hostility depends on a real and wholehearted pursuit of the glory and honour of God, rather than a concern for personal, family and sectional advantage. In other words, the soldier who is not sure of his allegiance is unlikely to serve well.

In the context of this whole section of Ephesians, righteousness similarly focuses mainly on doing the will of God – being righteous as he is and living that out in the details of life – rather than on the righteousness of Christ imputed to the believer, although the latter may not be entirely absent from Paul's thought here. In short, Christians fight Satan by the daily, conscious pursuit of inner truth and outer righteousness in every part of their lives. This also has implications for church life, where it may at times be necessary to pursue righteousness and truth as a community through the discipline of wayward members. There are New Testament reminders of the need to defend the church by the exercise of church discipline; the presence of sexual impurity, false teaching or the pursuit of party interest within a church all demand a conscious response if the church's testimony is not to be undermined (1 Cor. 5:1-13; 1 Tim. 1:18-20; Titus 3:9-11). Once again, the vital issue is that of recognising the 'depth' of the issues involved, which go beyond the particular individuals implicated in sin to the "spiritual forces of evil in the heavenly realms" which are using them for their own purposes.

Prayer

The concluding verses of the passage on spiritual armour focus on prayer. It is the ultimate and most vital weapon in the armoury of believers. Through it they recognize their dependence on God in the battle that confronts them, and come to him for the strength they need. Any army relies on supplies that come from its base. If those supplies are cut off, the army will be in deep trouble because it no longer has the resources it needs. In spiritual warfare the same principle applies. Christians are a pilgrim people in a hostile land, and so they are constantly dependent on resources that God alone can supply. For James too, responding to conflicts that were tearing the church apart and in which he recognized Satan's hand, drawing near to God and resisting the devil were two sides of the same coin:

> Submit yourselves, then, to God. Resist the devil, and
> he will flee from you. Come near to God and he will
> come near to you (James 4:7).

In the face of all that opposes them, it is only by God's help that believers can both stand fast against the devil, and also carry out the mission that God has given them. The response of God's people through the ages has always been the same:

> I lift up my eyes to the hills – where does my help come
> from? My help comes from the LORD, the Maker of
> heaven and earth (Ps. 121:1-2).

As they face the powers of darkness, therefore, Paul urges his readers to pray for themselves and "for all the saints" (Eph. 6:18).

The Lord Jesus Christ himself also emphasized the centrality of prayer in the struggle with Satan through both his teaching and his example. The prayer he taught his disciples is quite brief, but it is a model in which he teaches the essential elements and spirit of all truly Christian prayer. It is, therefore, significant that among the six or seven short petitions of the prayer, there is a request for deliverance from *evil*, an expression which may equally – and perhaps better – be understood as asking for deliverance from 'the evil one', Satan himself. Jesus' own experience had shown him that, as his disciples sought to follow him, strength to face their spiritual enemy was vital and would only come through communion with the Father. The same awareness is evident as he prays to his Father for them close to the end of his earthly ministry: "My prayer is not that you take them out of the world but that you protect them from the evil one" (John 17:15).

Probably the greatest test of his own life came as he contemplated the increasingly imminent event of the cross. John draws attention to his intense inner suffering when he reports Jesus' words,

> Now my heart is troubled, and what shall I say? 'Father, save me from this hour'? No, it was for this very reason I came to this hour. Father, glorify your name! (John 12:27-28).

In the garden of Gethsemane, the trial reached its highest point, when "being in anguish, he prayed more earnestly, and his sweat was like drops of blood falling to the ground" (Luke 22:44). The critical point here is the fact that in this climactic moment of grief and distress, unequalled in the experience of any other human being, his response was to pray. It was in praying that he found the strength he needed – and he overcame. Moreover, there is a striking contrast between his experience and that of the disciples – especially Peter, whose failure was that he did not recognize his own vulnerability. Jesus knew that it would be a time of great testing, not only for himself but also for his disciples, and so he urged them too to pray "that you will not fall into temptation" (Luke 22:40), echoing the last petition of the prayer he had taught them. He had already warned Peter specifically:

> Simon, Simon, Satan has asked to sift you as wheat. But I have prayed for you, Simon, that your faith may not fail. And when you have turned back, strengthen your brothers (Luke 22:31-32).

Peter's self-confident response shows that he did not realize his need of the grace of God in the trial he was about to face, "Lord, I am ready to go with you to prison and to death" (Luke 22:33). In the moment of crisis, however, he slept instead of praying, and fell more disastrously than all the other disciples.

It is not just Christian survival that depends on prayer, but the progress of the gospel. On the one hand, it is God who sends out labourers into his harvest, and those already engaged in the work are to pray that he would do so, for such labourers are always few (Matt. 9:37-38). On the other hand, those who are sent depend on God to supply both the ability and the courage to carry out the work they are called to do. Paul urged the Ephesians to pray for himself specifically in the context of his own mission, and at a time of special trial as he remained incarcerated in prison (Eph. 6:18-20; 1 Thess. 5:25). His emphasis on prayer for courage – "that I may fearlessly make known the mystery of the gospel . . . that I may declare it fearlessly" – is especially striking, and echoes the great apostolic prayer meeting following the arrest of Peter and John: "enable your servants to speak your word with great boldness" (Acts 4:29). Satan stirs fear in those who engage in mission, and prayer alone is the response to it. The notion of the missionary prayer letter is rooted in this same conviction – at least in principle, and if they are wise those who carry the gospel realize that prayer support is more critical than financial support. Paul recognized that relationships with governing authorities can be an arena of spiritual warfare, and he commanded prayer for rulers, particularly so that the church might experience peace and be able to continue in its mission (1 Tim. 2:2-4).

Prayer is an important response to situations of sickness, mentioned in James 5:14-15. Western approaches to sickness tend to emphasize the physical factors involved, while the African stress lies on the more 'spiritual' elements. A biblical perspective recognizes the reality of both the spiritual and physical dimensions, and the importance of each. The Bible does refer to the use of medicine: Jeremiah 8:22 assumes the existence of balm and physicians, while Exodus 21:18-19 implies the use, and expense, of medical care. The belief that illness and health came ultimately from God did not rule out use of medical procedures based on empirical research, any more than the recognition that God gives food should inhibit farming and the development of improved agricultural techniques. Nevertheless, it remains true that for the Bible, God is indeed the one in whose hands lie human health and sickness, and who finally determines the moment of death. Thus, in the face of sickness, prayer is no less important than medical care, and should be an unquestioned part of the Christian response to illness. Both Paul and Job prayed when they lost their health.

Nevertheless, neither of them sought to uncover spiritual forces of oppression. They did not engage in direct confrontation with Satan – there is indeed no evidence in the biblical text that Job ever knew or even suspected satanic involvement. Even less did they involve themselves in occult manipulation – such as consulting a diviner – to find healing. Throughout the book of Job, Job persistently brought his complaint into the presence of God alone: "I desire to speak to the Almighty and to argue my case with God" (Job 13:3). Similarly, while Paul recognized that the source of his "thorn in the flesh" was a "messenger from Satan", he did not try to deal with the demon directly but prayed to God, who gave him the answer, and finally contented himself with God's response – that the affliction would continue.

The same principle applies to cultural contexts in which witchcraft might be regarded as a potential source of suffering, where the aggression of a witch is immediately suspected in the case of any particular illness or accident. In such situations, the believer should turn directly to God, for whatever the source of an affliction might be – and the answer to that question is not ultimately important for the sufferer – God is the unique source of deliverance. This is a point of particular significance for those who might be tempted to use a diviner to identify the source of their ills, and then employ various occult medicines or rituals to bring about restoration of health. As we have said already, the pursuit of witches and direct engagement with evil spirits that supposedly cause illness are *not* a part of the Christian's spiritual warfare: Christians should not engage in witch-hunts, which have often been massively misconceived and at different times have caused huge suffering in Europe, America and Africa.

In a similar way, prayer is the vital resource as believers may face attack of an occult and demonic kind in the course of their ministries. In such circumstances, it may be particularly important to gather the church for prayer, or to inform colleagues and friends further afield of the need so that they can join in intercession. As we may encounter people who suffer demonic affliction of various sorts, including possession, prayer and fasting is the necessary response, as Jesus himself taught (Mark 9:29). The disciples' approach to possessed people was very simple: they invoked the name of Jesus and told the demon to leave (Acts 16:18). There does not seem to have been any other secret; like Jesus they did not use complex and exotic techniques. Nevertheless, it is vital to note that the effective use of the name of Jesus depends upon a real knowledge of him and relationship with him. His name is not at the disposition of those who would like to exploit it as a magic formula, as the sons of Sceva attempted to do with disastrous consequences (Acts 19:13-16). This is, once again, an example of using Satan's methods in the struggle, and so falling into his trap. In conclusion, we should also note that nobody is finally delivered from demonic power until they are also regenerated by the power of the Holy Spirit. If spirits are expelled from a person but not replaced by God's Spirit, then that person's final state risks being worse than the first (Matt. 12:43-45).

Weapons that overcome

Successful warfare is warfare that overcomes. In the celebration described by John in Revelation, after the coming of salvation and the defeat of the dragon, "a loud voice in heaven" identified three critical weapons by which "our brothers" overcame Satan:

> They overcame him by the blood of the Lamb and by
> the word of their testimony; they did not love their lives
> so much as to shrink from death (Rev. 12:11).

First, there is "the blood of the lamb". It is Christ's atoning death that redeems his people, freeing them from sin and so from slavery to Satan. Accordingly, in their warfare against him Christians must know first of all who they are in Christ – the position that they have received: that they are free from sin and, therefore, free from Satan too, and that they belong now to God and the Lord Jesus Christ. When Satan accuses and menaces them, they must be able to remind themselves once again of the reality of what they have become, and that the one who accuses has been "hurled down" from heaven once and for all. He no longer has any hold over those who belong to Christ. Christians need to see the world and Satan – indeed the whole of reality – from that perspective. In Christ, and because of his shed blood, they are already conquerors – they must know this, and it needs to shape their thinking and their lives. It is a foundational truth that believers are decisively freed from bondage to all the powers of darkness because of Christ:

> For he has rescued us from the dominion of darkness
> and brought us into the kingdom of the Son he loves,

in whom we have redemption, the forgiveness of sins
(Col. 1:13-14).

Once again, the text reminds us of the critical importance of
a clear and solid grasp of biblical truth, and so of a renewed
mind and worldview – and a renewed life.

Second, there is "the word of their testimony." The text
moves from the status that believers have in Christ to the
missionary task that has been conferred on them, and the
uniquely aggressive weapon that God has given them to carry
it out. They engage Satan through their testimony to the
gospel, and in doing so they overcome him. A crucial initial
point here is that the word of testimony is truth: Satan is a
liar and believers attack him with the truth that unmasks his
lies. In this way, gospel testimony responds to the blindness
of the human heart and frees men and women from the power
of the evil one:

> If you hold to my teaching, you are really my disciples.
> Then you will know the truth, and the truth will set you
> free (John 8:31-32).

The same point emerges in Paul's description of the spiritual
armour: "the sword of the Spirit" – the only piece of aggressive
armour he mentions – is the word of God. This is aggressive
spiritual warfare for, as they bear witness to truth, God's
people summon men and women to respond to Christ in
repentance and faith with the purpose of robbing Satan of
his possessions. This means that there is a 'power encounter'
every time that the word is faithfully preached.

Moreover, it is the same word of truth that brings
progressive sanctification to the people of God themselves
(John 17:17), reshaping their thinking and so transforming

their lives. It destroys Satan's strongholds in their minds, as well as in the minds of those they minister to (2 Cor. 10:4-5). It is vital to note that Christians engage in aggressive spiritual warfare through the communication of the word of God *alone*: the unique weapon of aggression that they possess is always spiritual and never physical.

Finally, "they did not love their lives so much as to shrink from death." The gospel advances through the messengers' total commitment to it, and their willingness to suffer for the sake of Christ. There is a profound principle of Christian life and ministry here. Jesus Christ accomplished his mission through crucifixion, and declared that following him similarly involved taking up the cross:

> If any man would come after me let him deny himself and take up his cross and follow me . . . he who saves his life shall lose it (Mark 8:34-35).

It is when the grain of wheat falls into the ground and dies that it produces fruit (John 12:24). Paul spoke of the afflictions that he endured for the sake of the church (Col. 1:24). In Revelation, believers are not promised deliverance from the trials and persecution that afflict them, but the crown of life if they persevere to the end.

There are two principal implications here. First, implicit in spiritual warfare there is the conscious dying to self and one's own interests: ". . . he must deny himself" (Matt. 16:24). It means the abandonment of personal ambitions, desires, needs, and whatever one might consider to be one's rights, for the sake of Christ and the gospel. Overcoming Satan means a readiness to die to self. Second, there is the willingness to accept the sufferings that come uninvited into one's life, maybe through satanic opposition and persecution. Satan makes war on the people of God, and sufferings are inevitable as they bear testimony to Christ. Throughout the history of the church this has been so, and especially at the great periods of expansion for the gospel: the early church, the Reformation, the missionary movement of recent centuries and so on. In the words of Dietrich Bonhoeffer, "When God calls a man he bids him come and die."[6] The warfare to which Christians are called involves dying rather than killing. There is no room here for easy discipleship, nor for a superficial triumphalism that expects victory without a cross and dreams of a life of ease, health and prosperity in the service of Christ. The amazing truth is that just as Christ overcame through death, so God's purposes continue to advance as his people take up the cross, and suffer and die for him. Death is the distinguishing feature of the advance of the true church of Jesus Christ in every age as it lives under the cross – "hacked to pieces, marked with scratches, despised, crucified, mocked."[7] This leads us to a final point.

A mighty army

Wars are not fought by individuals. It is true that in the Old Testament, David overcame Goliath, but his victory in single combat was quickly followed by the clash of the Israelite and Philistine armies. Alexander the Great, Julius Caesar, Napoleon and other great military leaders would have achieved nothing without the armies that followed them.

---

[6]D. Bonhoeffer, *The Cost of Discipleship* (London: SCM Press, 2001), 44.
[7]Martin Luther, *Table Talk*, in T. G. Tappert (ed. & translator), *Luther's Works*, Vol. 54 (Philadelphia: Fortress Press, 1967), 262.

The same is true of spiritual warfare, which is not simply concerned with the combat of individual Christians, but with the engagement of the whole people of God. This is one reason why Satan seeks to stir division within the church: divided armies lose battles.

Consequently, all that we have said in this chapter concerns not only individual believers but also the church as a body. The *church* must use spiritual weapons in its collective life and ministry; the *church* must pursue and foster a common intelligence – a shared worldview – that is shaped by the Scriptures and not by the culture of the surrounding world; the *church* must seek righteousness and truth in its life together; the *church* must engage in collective prayer in order to be sustained in its mission by the Spirit of God; and the *church* as a body must be rooted in Christ, focused on faithfully bearing witness, and ready to take up the cross and die.

In addition to all of this, however, the church must also be the source of training, encouragement and comfort for its individual members. Believers need to face Satan and the world together: it is in fellowship that they are able to stand before the enemy, while isolated soldiers are readily picked off. Therefore, they support one another and pray for one another, "contending as one man for the faith of the gospel" (Phil. 1:27). Where there are suspicions, disputes and animosities they help one another to achieve reconciliation, repentance and pardon (Phil. 4:2-3). Through the gifting and ministry of all the members, individual Christians and the whole church are built up "as each part does its work", until all come to maturity:

> Then we will no longer be infants, tossed back and forth
> by the waves, and blown here and there by every wind
> of teaching and by the cunning and craftiness of men
> in their deceitful scheming (Eph 4:14).

Necessarily, all of this means that the church must make the preservation of its own unity an absolute priority. We have already noted the multiple ways in which division can cripple churches. Faced with them all the church must seek to be a community of forbearance, forgiveness and reconciliation. It should be seeking to live out the reality of its nature as the redeemed and reconciled people of God – reconciled not only to God but also to one another. Witchcraft accusation breeds in an atmosphere of suspicion and conflict, and traditionally it was often the diviner who tried to repair the breakdowns in human relationships that led to such accusations. In the body of Christ believers and their leaders should themselves be active in so promoting reconciliation and forgiveness that the very language of witchcraft can gain no foothold.

In this context, a final, vital issue is the care that members should have for one another, and especially for those who succumb and fall in the conflict. It has been cynically, but not entirely falsely, said that the Christian church is the only army that shoots its own wounded. While discipline is without doubt a vital element of church life, as we have already noticed, there should also be a genuine concern for the casualties, and a desire for their repentance and restoration. It is only by grace that any are able to stand; and so,

> . . . if someone is caught in a sin, you who are spiritual
> should restore him gently. But watch yourself, or you
> also may be tempted (Gal. 6:1).

Conclusion

Ultimately, the battle is always God's. Most profoundly of all, the Bible teaches that God works even through the vilest of Satan's deeds. Evil never ever wins. What may appear to be defeat and disaster can turn out to be a means of blessing and victory. The greatest crime ever committed in human history must surely have been the crucifixion of Jesus Christ, the Lord of glory. The New Testament indicates that Satan conspired to bring it about (Luke 22:3,53; John 13:2,27), and yet it was through that same cross – Satan's ultimate crime – that he and all his forces were disarmed and decisively defeated (Col. 2:15), and his captives were freed. In the same way, the persecution that followed the martyrdom of Stephen brought about the massive expansion of the church as believers were scattered and took the gospel wherever they went (Acts 8:1-4). The dispute between Paul and Barnabas which seems to be so tragic, actually led to the mobilisation of two missionary enterprises in place of just one (Acts 15:39-40). The overcoming of occult opposition in Acts 13, and the discomfiture of the sons of Sceva in Acts 19, both resulted in a positive response to the gospel (13:12; 19:17-20). Paul wrote several of his epistles during his imprisonment, to the lasting blessing of churches everywhere down through the centuries. During the same time he was also able to witness to his gaolers while his example encouraged other Christians in their witness too (Phil. 1:12-14).

Such a reflection should not make us complacent about evil, and certainly not fatalistic, but it assures us that the victory of our Saviour is certain. He will build his church; he will rescue his own from every evil attack; and he will bring them safely to his heavenly kingdom (2 Tim. 4:18). Christians may take heart, for he has overcome the world (John 16:33).

Questions for further reflection

1. "... God is faithful; he will not let you be tempted beyond what you can bear. But when you are tempted, he will also provide a way out so that you can stand up under it" (1 Cor. 10:13). What are the 'ways out' which God provides?

2. What inappropriate 'warfare' have you met among Christians?

3. How can we foster the renewing of our minds (Rm. 12:2)?

4. Why is prayerlessness so widespread among Christians?

5. "When God calls a man he bids him come and die": how have you 'died' as a believer, and why?

CHAPTER 7

CONCLUSION

The LORD reigns, let the earth be glad;
let the distant shores rejoice.
Clouds and thick darkness surround him;
righteousness and justice are the foundation
of his throne.
Fire goes before him
and consumes his foes on every side.
His lightning lights up the world;
the earth sees and trembles.
The mountains melt like wax before the LORD,
before the Lord of all the earth.
The heavens proclaim his righteousness,
and all the peoples see his glory.
—Psalm 97:1-6

The notion of 'total warfare' is a relatively recent one in human history. It refers to massive conflicts in which every area of national life is focused on the war effort. Thus all economic resources, the whole population, every dimension of social and political life are mobilized to bring victory over the enemy – or at least to ensure national survival. However, in spiritual terms the warfare in which Christians are engaged against the world, the devil and the remains of indwelling sin, has always been 'total'. There is no area of life free from attack by the enemies of God and his people. Home and family, work and social life, the church – all are exposed to his assaults in one way or another, and vigilance is constantly and everywhere necessary. As Peter reminded his readers, "Be self-controlled and alert. Your enemy the devil prowls around like a roaring lion looking for someone to devour" (1 Pet. 5:8). It is important, therefore, not to confine the battle to certain areas alone – to the conflict with demon possession, for example, or with witches and sorcerers. These are, in fact, relatively minor theatres of spiritual warfare: the reality is that every aspect of the Christian's life is one of combat, and the devil's aim is the destruction of the work of God and, more specifically, of the believer's faith and testimony. It is not a phenomenon known only to certain Christians, or experienced only in certain churches or places or cultures. We may face different issues according to our cultural or historical setting, but ultimately we are all engaged in the same warfare and we must all employ the same weapons.

Nevertheless, we also need to recognize the danger of overstating the threat that Satan and his forces pose to the people of God. The great reality is that God is sovereign, that Christ is the conqueror of every enemy, and that the Holy Spirit of God indwells every Christian believer. There is a need for a biblical balance and realism, as there is in all areas of Christian life and experience. One aspect of that balance is recognising that the Bible actually does not say so very much about Satan and the powers of darkness. At no point, for example, does it give us any sort of detailed analysis of the spirit world. We do not know the differences – if indeed there are differences – between powers and authorities and thrones, or between fallen angels and unclean spirits. Consequently, there are issues that have not been discussed in this book, questions that remain unanswered, because the answers are not given to us. There is an implicit warning here against delving into matters that God has decided not to reveal. We are told enough for our good and for our spiritual security and progress; but we are not told all that our curiosity might want to know. In this area it is unhealthy and dangerous to go beyond what is written for us.

Returning to the issue with which we started this study, peoples of almost every society have conceptions of the unseen world – the world of spirits and occult power – and those conceptions are culturally defined. There is a tendency to read the Bible in the light of them, and so to distort the biblical witness. Rather, what needs to happen is that we should submit our culturally shaped ideas and beliefs to evaluation by the Word of God, and allow them to be changed where necessary. This is not only true of the invisible world, but in fact of every aspect of our lives and experience. However, in the African context in which ancestors, spirits and sorcerers are such a significant part of the reality that people have come to know, it is particularly important to submit that dimension of life to the judgement of God's word, and to allow it to transform minds – and so to transform lives.

For almost every culture, a common feature of belief in a world of spirits and unseen forces is fear. Satan himself has an interest in stoking such fears, and so paralysing believers in their service for God as to make them useless. He wants to shut them up in rooms that are locked out of fear of what may be waiting for them outside – somewhat like the situation of the disciples just after the crucifixion and resurrection of Jesus. However, Christ's purpose is always to bring peace where there is fear, to empower his people through his Spirit, and to send them into the world to bring the message of God's grace to lost men and women (John 20:19-23). What God reveals in the Bible responds to every fear. Believers may be weak in themselves – far weaker indeed than Satan, but they have a sovereign God and a victorious, risen Saviour, with whom they are already seated in the heavenly realms. The final truth is that

> . . . neither angels nor demons . . . nor any powers . . .
> nor anything else in all creation, will be able to separate
> us from the love of God that is in Christ Jesus our Lord
> (Rom. 8:38-39).

And so, to conclude with the words, once more, of Martin Luther:

> *We win no battles through our might,*
> *we fall at once dejected*
> *the righteous one will lead the fight*
> *by God himself directed.*
> *You ask, 'Who can this be?',*
> *Christ Jesus, it is he*
> *eternal King and Lord,*
> *God's true and living Word,*
> *one can stand against Him.*[1]

---

[1]Martin Luther, *Ein' Feste Burg ist unser Gott*, translated by Stephen Orchard, in Edwards et al (eds.), *Praise!*, 888.

FURTHER READING

Arnold, C. E., *Powers of Darkness* (Leicester: IVP, 1992).

Burnett, D., *Unearthly Powers* (Eastbourne: Marc, 1988).

Carson, D. A., *How Long, O Lord: Reflections on Suffering and Evil* (Leicester: Inter-Varsity Press, 1990).

De Villiers, P. G. R. (ed.), *Like a roaring lion ...: Essays on the Bible, the church and demonic powers* (Pretoria: C.B. Powell Bible Centre, University of South Africa, 1987).

Evans-Pritchard, E.E., *Witchcraft, Oracles and Magic among the Azande* (Oxford: Clarendon Press, 1976 [1937]).

Ferdinando, K., *The Triumph of Christ in African Perspective: a Study of Demonology and Redemption in the African Context* (Carlisle: Paternoster, 1999).

Gehman, R., *African Traditional Religion in Biblical Perspective* (Nairobi: East African Educational Publishers, 2005).

Hiebert, P. G., *Transforming Worldviews: An Anthropological Understanding of How People Change* (Grand Rapids: Baker, 2008).

Hiebert, P. G., Shaw, D. R., Tiénou, T., *Understanding Folk Religion* (Grand Rapids: Baker, 1999).

Leahy, F. S., *Satan Cast Out: A Study in Biblical Demonology* (Edinburgh: Banner of Truth Trust, 1975).

Lloyd-Jones, D. M., *The Christian Warfare: an Exposition of Ephesians 6:10-13* (Edinburgh: The Banner of Truth Trust, 1976).

Longman, T. and Reid, D. G., *God is a Warrior* (Grand Rapids: Zondervan, 1995).

Marwick, M. (ed.), *Witchcraft and Sorcery* (Harmondsworth: Penguin Books, 1990).

Mbiti, J.S., *African Religions and Philosophy* (Oxford: Heinemann, 1969).

Moreau, A. S., *The World of the Spirits: a Biblical Study in the African Context* (Nairobi: Evangel Publishing House, 1990).

O'Brien, P. T., 'Principalities and Powers: Opponents of the Church' in
    D.A. Carson (ed.), *Biblical Interpretation and the Church: the Problem
    of Contextualisation* (Nashville, Tennessee: Nelson, 1985).
Page, S. H. T., *Powers of Evil* (Grand Rapids and Leicester: Baker and
    Apollos, 1995).
Parrinder, E.G., *African Traditional Religion* (London: Sheldon Press,
    1974).
Powlison, D., *Power Encounters: Reclaiming Spiritual Warfare* (Grand
    Rapids: Baker, 1995).
Yamauchi, E. M., 'Magic in the Biblical World', *TB 34* (1983).

ACTS PUBLICATIONS

Advanced New Testament Greek	Helleman & Gava
African Christian Theology,	Aben
African Indigenous Churches.	Ayegboyin & Ishola
African Traditional Religion in the Light of the Bible,	Gehman
AIDS is Real and it's in our Church,	Garland & Blyth
Bible Women.	Ekanem
Biblical Preaching in Africa,	Janvier
Biblical Theology of Missions,	Fuller
Celebrating Life,	McCain
Christian Ethics,	Shields
Christianity and Islam,	Abashiya & Ulea
Christianity in Northern Nigeria,	Crampton (update by Gaiya)
Christians in Politics,	Danladi Musa
Churches in Fellowship: The Story of TEKAN,	Hopkins & Gaiya
Cross-cultural Christianity,	Hassan, et al.
Culture and the Christian Home (2nd Ed),	Kore
Discipleship: a West African Perspective,	Janvier & Thaba
Essentials of Christian Religious Studies in Colleges of Ed,	Wiebe, et al, (3 vols.)
Every Abortion Stops a Beating Heart,	Garland & Idoko
Exposition of First Corinthians for Today,	Yamsat

Textbooks for Theological Education in Africa: An Annotated Bibliography,	Starcher & Anguandia
Times of Refreshing: History of Revival in Africa,	Burgess
The Battle is God's	Ferdinando
The Bible and Islam.	Madany
The Work of the Missionary.	Fuller
Theology of the New Testament	Palmer
Theology of the Old Testament,	Palmer
Theology of Worship,	Bartlett
Tough Tests for Top Leaders,	McCain
Train to Teach Others,	Kure
Training for Church Planters.	Janvier
True Minister of God,	Onukwa
Truths for Healthy Churches,	Kore
Turn the Other Cheek,	Kadala
Two Models of Leadership,	McCain
Understanding & Applying the Scriptures,	McCain & Keener
Understanding the Bible,	Stott
Understanding Leadership,	Janvier/Thaba
What A Mess.	Timbuak
We Believe: Introduction on Christian Doctrine,	McCain (2 vols.)
You Could Be a Missionary,	Adekoya

ACTS / HippoBooks / Zondervan titles

African Christian Ethics	Kunhiyop
African Christian Theology	Kunhiyop
God, Where Are You?	Kisoni
Guide to Interpreting Scripture	Kyomya
My Neighbour's Faith (Islam Explained)	Azumah
Preachers of a Different Gospel	Adeleye
The Trinity of Sin	Turaki
The War Within	Chukwuocha

Africa Bible Commentary Series
(ACTS / HippoBooks / Zondervan)

1 & 2 Timothy and Titus	Ngewa
Galatians	Ngewa
Jeremiah and Lamentations	Bungishabaku
Romans	Andria